OTHER SIDE
OF THE GAME

OTHER SIDE
OF THE GAME

BY AMANDA PARRIS

PLAYWRIGHTS CANADA PRESS
TORONTO

Other Side of the Game © Copyright 2019 by Amanda Parris

LIBRARY AND ARCHIVES CANADA CATALOGUING IN PUBLICATION
Title: Other side of the game / Amanda Parris.
Names: Parris, Amanda, author.
Description: First edition. | A play.
Identifiers: Canadiana (print) 20190082488 | Canadiana (ebook) 20190082496 | ISBN 9781770919914 (softcover) | ISBN 9781770919921 (PDF) | ISBN 9781770919938 (EPUB) | ISBN 9781770919945 (Kindle)
Classification: LCC PS8631.A7669 O84 2019 | DDC C812/.6—dc23

Playwrights Canada Press acknowledges that we operate on land, which, for thousands of years, has been the traditional territories of the Mississaugas of the Credit First Nation, Huron-Wendat, Anishinaabe, Métis, and Haudenosaunee peoples. Today, this meeting place is home to many Indigenous peoples from across Turtle Island and we are grateful to have the opportunity to work and play here.

We acknowledge the financial support of the Canada Council for the Arts—which last year invested $153 million to bring the arts to Canadians throughout the country—the Ontario Arts Council (OAC), Ontario Creates, and the Government of Canada for our publishing activities.

Canada Council
for the Arts
Conseil des arts
du Canada

ONTARIO ARTS COUNCIL
CONSEIL DES ARTS DE L'ONTARIO
an Ontario government agency
un organisme du gouvernement de l'Ontario

ONTARIO | ONTARIO
CREATES | CRÉATIF

This play is dedicated to the women who trusted me with their stories. This work has always been first and foremost for you.

INTRODUCTION

Toronto is not good at remembering. As a city, and per-
haps also as a country, we have nurtured a culture of
forgetfulness, where what is new is vaulted and celebrated
often at the expense of the very things that built the
foundation for that emergence. This play is an attempt to
remember, re-centre and reconsider what and who often
gets forgotten.

Other Side of the Game was inspired by a personal
experience. Several years ago, I sat in the visitors' waiting
room of the Don Jail to see a friend who was incarcerated.
As I observed the women sitting beside me and across from
me, questions began floating through my mind. Who were
these women? Where had they come from? How were they
feeling? And why had I never heard their stories? I began
asking some of these women questions and they told me
about themselves, the men they loved and what that love
looked like when one person lived behind bars. In most
movies and TV shows, these women would be cast as the
supporting character to a male lead. I wanted to put them
centre stage.

Other Side of the Game was galvanized by a history of activism that has been wiped from the collective memory of this city. While I was reading Assata and Elaine and Afeni, immersing myself in the stories of the US Black Power Movement, I had no idea that my work as a community organizer in Toronto was only possible because of Akua and Makeda and Ayanna. I knew nothing about the rich and nuanced history of Black activism here. I wanted to put stories inspired by those women centre stage.

Other Side of the Game was initially dreamed up with the brilliant poet Keisha-Monique Simpson. It was our research, ideas and shared passion that helped to carve out the skeleton of the story and the initial sketches of these characters. In the first draft of the play, Keisha-Monique wrote beautiful dream sequences. They are not in this final version, but they were the first step in discovering the abstract, tension-riddled space of the waiting room that anchors this story.

Finally, *Other Side of the Game* is an archive of Toronto's soundscape. It may not be recognizable to every resident, but for those who reside in particular neighbourhoods it is a familiar salute, an act of acknowledgement and evidence of who was here and how they sounded.

Amanda Parris, May 2019

NOTES FROM THE PLAYWRIGHT

GENERAL BACKGROUND

In order to develop a road map for this story, I conducted interviews with thirteen individuals who connect to either side of the play: the radical political organizers of the '70s and '80s or the Hip Hop Generation that valorized and celebrated the prototype of the "ride-or-die chick."

The people that I interviewed for this play include women who have been incarcerated, women who support loved ones who are incarcerated and individuals who were heavily involved in radical political organizing in the '70s and '80s in Canada. The interviews were my key source material; however, this is not a verbatim theatre production. Real events are confused with memory, imagined histories and mystical elements. Characters are composites of real and fictional people.

THE WAITING ROOM

The waiting room represents a marked shift from the rest of the play. The choreographed cycles within it represent a form of purgatory. The entire company is in the waiting room. In the opening scene they all face the audience. In the second waiting room scene, only Nicole and Beverly face out while the rest of the company have their backs to the audience.

A sentence of movements is a phrase of ten choreographed gestures rooted in the idea of waiting (i.e., scratching, stretching, yawning) with an unanticipated scream of frustration that serves as the ultimate punctuation mark. In the waiting room everyone goes through the sentence of gestures, but they must always return to the neutral stasis of waiting and staring at the audience. In doing so they ensure that, despite the release that may come from the burst, the return to stasis makes every movement and scream ultimately unsatisfying.

CASTING

All of the characters who represent the system (guard, police officer, guidance counsellor and daycare workers) can be cast as Black, Indigenous or people of colour.

Other Side of the Game was first produced by Cahoots
Theatre Company and Obsidian Theatre Company in
October 2017 at the Aki Studio Theatre, Toronto, with the
following cast and creative team:

Virgilia Griffith
Shakura Dickson
Ryan Rosery
Peter Bailey
Ordena Stephens-Thompson

Directed by Nigel Shawn Williams
Set and Prop Design by Joanna Yu
Costume Design by Rachel Forbes
Lighting Design by Kaitlin Hickey
Sound Design by Verne Good
Choreography by Jasmyn Fyffe
Dramaturgy by Marjorie Chan
Production Management by Laura Warren
Stage Management by Neha Ross

Deaf Community Consultation by Symara Bonner
Deaf Interpretation by Samreen Aziz and Charlene Malone
ASL/English Interpretation by Tara Lee Everett and Erin
Fremlin

CHARACTERS

Beverly: Twenty-two-year-old Black Nova Scotian student.
Nicole: Twenty-one-year-old mother of Caribbean descent living in a Toronto hood.
Khalil: Twenty-five-year-old activist and student.
Akilah: Twenty-five-year-old activist and mother.
Devonte: Twenty-one-year-old of Caribbean descent caught up in the game.
Shevon: Twenty-one-year-old biracial young woman from a middle-class Toronto suburb.
Winston: Thirty-year-old drug dealer of Caribbean descent.
Elder: A sixty-year-old or older community organizer of Caribbean descent.
Officer #1 and #2
Guard
Ms. Flynn
Worker #1, #2 and #3

ROLES ARE DOUBLED AS FOLLOWS

One actor plays Beverly and Shevon
One actor plays Nicole and Akilah
One actor plays Khalil and Devonte
One actor plays Elder, Winston and Officer #1
One actor plays Officer #2, Ms. Flynn and Workers
One actor does the voice-over for Guard

SCENE 1

We are in the visitors' waiting room of the Don Jail in Toronto. It is filled with people sitting and waiting on hard chairs; they are the anonymous, faceless majority. They begin staring silently at the audience. This moment is pushed to the point of discomfort for the audience. The visitors suddenly erupt in a scream that expresses the pent-up frustration of their position. They perform a silent sentence of movements, sometimes independently and other times in unison. Each visitor is oblivious to the presence of the other, all existing in solitary isolation.

GUARD   ID please.
NICOLE   Yep. Here you go.

She passes him her ID.

GUARD	Miss, this is not valid identification.
NICOLE	What do you mean not va—
GUARD	Do you have anything else?
NICOLE	Like what?
GUARD	A driver's licence perhaps?
NICOLE	No. I don't drive.
GUARD	Passport?
NICOLE	Not on me. But that's my health card.
GUARD	Yeah, I can see that.
NICOLE	I spent two hours in a line getting it.
GUARD	Uh-huh.
NICOLE	And you're telling me it's not valid?
GUARD	Yup.
NICOLE	But—
GUARD	Listen, a health card is not considered valid ID. End of story. I'm sorry. You won't be able to come in today.
NICOLE	But—
GUARD	Next!

NICOLE turns around and now has her back to the audience. Simultaneously BEVERLY turns to face the audience.

	I'm sorry, ma'am, but we've been placed on lockdown. All visits are cancelled for the day.
BEVERLY	Lockdown?
GUARD	Yeah. Lockdown.
BEVERLY	But I called first and everything was fine.
GUARD	Uh-huh.
BEVERLY	I spent over an hour in traffic trying to get here!

GUARD   There's nothing I can do, ma'am.

BEVERLY   But—

GUARD   Try again another day. Next!

BEVERLY turns around and now has her back to the audience. Simultaneously NICOLE turns to face the audience.

Do you have any narcotics, food or electronics on you?

NICOLE   No . . . wait, yes.

GUARD   You are in current possession of narcotics?

NICOLE   No! Just . . . my cellphone.

GUARD   You can't bring that on the premises.

NICOLE   So, what am I supposed to do with it? Do you guys have lockers or something?

GUARD   Not at this facility, miss. You can put it in your car and line up again.

NICOLE   I don't have a car!

GUARD   Hmph.

NICOLE   And I just stood in line for twenty minutes.

GUARD   Okay.

NICOLE   Okay? So . . . what am I supposed to do?

GUARD   I don't know what you're supposed to do. I just know what I'm supposed to do. And I cannot allow you in with that cellphone.

NICOLE   But—

GUARD   Next!

NICOLE turns around and now has her back to the audience. Simultaneously BEVERLY turns to face the audience.

	Sorry, ma'am, we're not letting any more visitors in for the day.
BEVERLY	But it's 3:30.
GUARD	Yeah, I can see that.
BEVERLY	Visiting hours are until four.
GUARD	Yes but you need to arrive with ample time for us to locate the inmate and bring them in from their range.
BEVERLY	That's ridiculous. How much time could you really need? . . .
GUARD	I'm sorry but you'll have to come back another day.
BEVERLY	But—
GUARD	*(rapidly)* Numbers thirty-one, forty-eight, twenty-one, nineteen and eighty-two.
BEVERLY	Did they say thirty-nine?
NICOLE	Did you call thirty-nine?
GUARD	You should have listened when the numbers were announced.
NICOLE	I know but I couldn't hear.
GUARD	Well that's your problem. Maybe you should pay attention next time.

Both BEVERLY and NICOLE kiss their teeth.

SCENE 2

*We are in an office where Black activists
do political work somewhere in Toronto.
AKILAH sits at a typewriter with piles of file
folders and papers beside her. She is rapidly
typing. KHALIL is seated reading a book in a
separate area from AKILAH and jotting down
ideas in a notebook.*

KHALIL   Well if we incorporate some of James's analysis
         on the dialectic that might address the gap.

AKILAH   Mmm-hmm . . .

KHALIL   Do you think it's directly applicable?

AKILAH   Ummm—

KHALIL   I mean it might piss some folks off . . .

AKILAH   It might . . .

KHALIL   But we can use it to illustrate—

AKILAH   Khalil, can you—

KHALIL   What?

AKILAH   I'm trying to edit this brief, but you keep
          talking and it's making me type what you're
          saying instead of—
KHALIL   So? You can't do two things at once?

> *AKILAH sighs and KHALIL gets up and walks towards her.*

Hey why you getting so heavy? You need some
help? What are you working on?

> *He leans over her shoulder, peering at what she's typing.*

AKILAH   The briefing on the New Jewel Movement.
KHALIL   Oh yes.

> *He moves in closer.*

Mmmm. You smell good.

> *AKILAH kisses her teeth.*

AKILAH   Khalil.
KHALIL   What? You do! What are you wearing?
AKILAH   Just . . . stop.

> *She gets up.*

KHALIL   Why you so uptight? I was just—

The door opens suddenly and BEVERLY *hesitatingly steps into the room.*

BEVERLY Hi.

AKILAH Can I help you?

KHALIL Why is that door unlocked?

BEVERLY Sorry to—

KHALIL brushes past BEVERLY *and locks the door.*

I'm Beverly. I called earlier and spoke to . . .

She consults her notebook.

. . . ummm . . . a Brother Kwame?

AKILAH He just stepped out.

BEVERLY Oh. He told me to come by because . . . well, I was wondering if I would be able to sign up . . . you know to join the Movement?

AKILAH I see. Well, come in if you're coming in.

BEVERLY sits across from AKILAH.

Khalil, do you mind finishing off these edits?

A pause as KHALIL *looks at* AKILAH *as if she's joking.*

Or you can print the student outreach flyers or finish the clinic budget or reorganize the new books for the library. Your choice.

There is a tense moment before KHALIL
walks over and sits at AKILAH's *desk. He eyes*
BEVERLY *suspiciously before starting to type.*
His typing is much slower than AKILAH's.

Thank you. Okay, so . . . we generally don't
allow people to just walk in and join the
Movement. We have to exercise caution about
who is allowed within our ranks. I'm sure you
understand.

BEVERLY Yes of course.

AKILAH What was your name again?

BEVERLY Beverly.

AKILAH I'm Akilah and this is Brother Khalil. So . . .
what do you do?

BEVERLY What do I do? Uhhh . . . well I'm a student. I
just transferred to York.

AKILAH Where were you before?

BEVERLY Concordia. But I grew up in Halifax.

AKILAH What's your major?

BEVERLY I'm undecided right now. I'm just taking a
bunch of courses. I spent half the semester at
Carleton doing journalism but it wasn't a good
fit. So now I'm just trying different things.

AKILAH Concordia, Carleton, York . . . still undecided.
You've been bouncing around quite a bit.

BEVERLY Yeah. I guess I have.

AKILAH So what work have you done for the Movement
previously?

BEVERLY Umm well . . . back home, my parents were
involved in the whole Africville thing, so I was
around a lot of that and I used to go to Kwacha

	House sometimes and listen to, you know, the talks they had. I'm also a poet kind of . . . I write a lot . . . I don't know if that counts.
KHALIL	It doesn't.
AKILAH	Who were your parents working with on the Africville movement?
BEVERLY	Ummm do you mean specific people? It was all happening through our church so . . .
AKILAH	Hm.
BEVERLY	I know churches are not the most forward thinking—
AKILAH	Not at all.
BEVERLY	—but in my community, they were kind of the hub of everything and—
KHALIL	Do you identify yourself as a backward, cultural nationalist only willing to commit to kente cloth and Egyptology? Or are you a revolutionary?
BEVERLY	What? No . . . I'm a . . . well I want to be a revolutionary.
KHALIL	Do you know what it means to be a revolutionary?
BEVERLY	It means to—
KHALIL	A Black Revolutionary?
BEVERLY	It means I'm ready to fight . . . fight the man . . . for my people.
KHALIL	The man? No, Kimberly—
BEVERLY	It's Beverly—
KHALIL	Whatever. To be a Black Revolutionary means that you have declared war.
BEVERLY	War? Like the war in Vietnam?

KHALIL	No. Not that war. This is a war on anyone and anything that believes it can rape our women, castrate our men and miseducate our children. It means you have enlisted in a war on the rich who can only stay rich when they keep us poor. It means you have declared war on the fascist politricksters who lie to us while grinning their teeth in our faces. To be a Black Revolutionary means that you declare war on the colonizers and capitalists who steal and plunder and destroy land that belongs to the Indian people of this earth.
BEVERLY	Oh. Yeah. That's what I meant.
KHALIL	Oh that's what you meant? Man don't be coming to me with all this jive—
AKILAH	Take it easy, Khalil.
KHALIL	I'll ask you again. Are you, Sister, a Black Revolutionary?
BEVERLY	I am a Black Revolutionary.
AKILAH	Are you a socialist, Sister Beverly?
BEVERLY	Ummm . . . yes.
KHALIL	What have you studied?
BEVERLY	Studied?
KHALIL	Trotsky? Mao? James? Althusser?
BEVERLY	Well umm no . . . I haven't gotten around to . . .
KHALIL	So then how do you know you're a socialist?
BEVERLY	Well I got this pamphlet back at—
KHALIL	A pamphlet? These are crucial times. You cannot be caught sleeping.
BEVERLY	I'm not sleeping! I just . . . I thought that being a revolutionary meant . . . never mind. Right on!

KHALIL and AKILAH look at each other.

KHALIL   The sister isn't ready.

AKILAH   Be cool.

KHALIL   We have to remain vigilant. Look at the threat we're under!

AKILAH   I know that but don't persecute her for not knowing.

KHALIL   We don't have time for those that do not know.

AKILAH   That's exactly who we have to make time for.

KHALIL   She could be a spy for all we know.

BEVERLY   I'm not a—

KHALIL raises a hand to silence her.

KHALIL   Right now the stakes are high and therefore our standards must be high.

AKILAH   Everyone has to start somewhere. She'll learn.

BEVERLY   I will! Please. That's why I'm here. I'm frustrated and angry and I'm tired of feeling powerless. I just . . . I have so many questions—I'm so hungry to learn. It's why I came to Toronto but . . . maybe it was a mistake. I can't even find a place to stay. I just . . . I need to do something. You guys are doing something. I want to be a part of that.

AKILAH   Okay. You can join us, but you have a lot to learn. We'll begin with a detailed study plan. Every Wednesday evening we hold political education meetings at Third World Books and Crafts. If you're serious about this, you need to attend them. And I can help you find a place to stay.

BEVERLY   Right on, comrades. Thank you so much. You will not regret this.

She gets up to leave.

KHALIL   One last thing, Kimberly.

AKILAH   Khalil. Her name is Beverly.

KHALIL   Beverly.

BEVERLY   Yes, Brother Khalil?

KHALIL   Don't come back in here with that white man's red stain on your lips. We don't have time for that mess when we're fighting for revolution.

There's a knock at the door.

Yeah?

OFFICER   Police. Open up.

KHALIL and AKILAH look at each other. KHALIL answers the door but blocks the entryway with his body. The OFFICER cannot be seen.

KHALIL   Yes?

OFFICER   We've received some noise complaints and I'd like to look around.

KHALIL   Noise complaints from whom?

OFFICER   The other tenant in the building.

KHALIL   Is that so? I could have sworn Mr. Cadore was on vacation.

OFFICER   I'm not trying to start any trouble, I just want
           to look around, and if you have nothing to
           hide, it shouldn't be a problem.

KHALIL   I'm also not trying to start any trouble but I'm
           afraid you will not be able to look around.

OFFICER   Please, sir, don't make this more difficult than
           it needs to be.

KHALIL   If memory serves me correctly, according to the
           precedent set just five years ago in the 1974 case
           Knowlton v. the Crown, the Waterfield Test is
           the legal standard for search and seizure. Isn't
           that right, Sister Akilah?

AKILAH   That's correct, Brother Khalil. Under the
           Waterfield Test, an officer would need to prove
           to a judge that they conducted this search in
           order to investigate a crime, maintain order,
           ensure public safety or to keep the peace.

KHALIL   That's what I thought. So, Officer, do you
           think—given Mr. Cadore's absence, the pres-
           ence of two witnesses attesting to the peace and
           order of the premises and the fact that this is
           private property—do you really think that you
           would be able to prove all of that in a court of
           law? Because please believe we would be taking
           this to a court of law.

           Silence.

OFFICER   You're just making this harder on yourself.

KHALIL   Am I? I thought I was just following the letter
           of the law. Has the law changed since I last
           checked or . . . did it just change for me?

OFFICER	Unbelievable. This isn't America you know. You've got it good here.
KHALIL	Oh really? Did America kill Albert Johnson and Buddy Evans? I know where I am. Good day, Officer.
OFFICER	I'll be keeping an eye on you.
KHALIL	I'm sure you already are.

KHALIL closes the door and he and AKILAH look at each other again.

BEVERLY	Wow. Can you teach me how to do that?

SCENE 3

We are at a basketball court in a Toronto community. SHEVON *enters talking on the phone and sits down on a park bench.*

SHEVON   Ke-ke, you're not taking it in . . . I don't business. You said Friday so I cleared out my Friday accordingly. Nah, man, I got runs to make Saturday. Friday. No. I don't care. I done bought the hair.

NICOLE enters looking at her phone.

Hold on. Nicole!

SHEVON beckons NICOLE over.

What'd you say? Okay. That works. I'll be at your house by three.

NICOLE stands next to the bench.

	Whaddup?
NICOLE	Nothing.
SHEVON	Where you coming from? You never come this way.
NICOLE	Just dropped Zakiya at my gran, gotta go get some groceries.
SHEVON	Oh yeah? Since you're free, wanna deal with a ting?
NICOLE	No.
SHEVON	No? What's wrong wit you?
NICOLE	Seriously, Shevon? Zakiya's appointment was on Monday. You said you would drive us.
SHEVON	Shit. I totally forgot. Yo my bad.
NICOLE	Your bad for real. I actually got worried. I called you like ten times. You can't keep doing this.
SHEVON	I know, I know.
NICOLE	"We are women. Everything we do matters. I am not my sister's keeper. I am my sister."
SHEVON	Huh?
NICOLE	Iyanla Vanzant.
SHEVON	Nicole, how many times I gotta tell you—no one knows what the hell you're talking about when you start spitting all those inspiration quotes.
NICOLE	That's not true.
SHEVON	And Iyanla Vanzant don't know shit about me.
NICOLE	Don't cuss Iyanla. I just get worried.
SHEVON	I know but I already told you that you don't need to. I was with Winston and he would never let anything happen to me.

NICOLE sits down.

NICOLE   Hmph.

SHEVON   Don't even. I'm sorry about missing the appointment. I've just been mad busy. I'm on that grind right now. You know how it is.

NICOLE   That grind huh?

SHEVON   Yeah, you know, just out here tryna make that paper.

NICOLE   Riiight. If memory serves me correctly, don't you already get that paper through a weekly allowance?

SHEVON   Yo fall back.

NICOLE   I'm just saying . . .

SHEVON   Why you always bringing that up?

NICOLE   I'm just pointing out the obvious—

SHEVON   That was then and this is now.

NICOLE   Okay fine.

SHEVON   Fine.

NICOLE   Just don't go ghost again. I get worried and start thinking I might have to go find certain mans and . . . you know?

SHEVON   Yeah, I know. How'd it go at the appointment?

NICOLE   Fine. It was just an ear infection thank goodness. The prescription was so friggin expensive.

SHEVON   You said no before, but if you want to get in on this—

NICOLE   No. I don't. It'll work out. Paulo Coelho says—

SHEVON   Who?

NICOLE   Paulo Coelho.

SHEVON   Paulo from Chalkfarm?

NICOLE   No. He's this—

SHEVON	Paulo from Trimbee?
NICOLE	Nah, man. A writer from Brazil—
SHEVON	Oh. Right, right.
NICOLE	He says "Only three things can change our lives: dreams, suffering and love." Hopefully this means change is coming.
SHEVON	Yeaaah. How about we go out this weekend? Get your mind offa all this.
NICOLE	Shevon, I just said I have no money.
SHEVON	Come on. I got you. We'll go to that little club at Jane and Wilson.
NICOLE	I can't. I don't have a babysitter.
SHEVON	Just leave him with your granny.
NICOLE	Nah, man. Now that he's crawling, he's getting way too fast for her. It's too much with all her arthritis and shit.
SHEVON	It'll be late. He'll probably be sleeping. Your grandmother won't have to run around.

NICOLE sighs.

NICOLE	Jane and Wilson? Why you always dragging me to these little dugga-dugga spots for?
SHEVON	Because the hood is where you get the best music and the cheapest drinks. Besides, you know Poochie runs that place now, right?
NICOLE	Poochie from Martha?
SHEVON	Nah he moved—
NICOLE	Poochie from Driftwood?
SHEVON	Eeew no—
NICOLE	Poochie from Falstaff?

SHEVON   That's the one, and if you show up there look-
          ing like a sweeter ting, you know him and his
          thirsty ass will be hookin us up with mad bot-
          tles for the night!

          They both laugh. DEVONTE *enters, sees*
          NICOLE *and pauses, taken aback. He checks
          her out and then sneaks up behind them.*

          Truss me. It'll be live. Just like old times.
NICOLE   I'll think about it.
DEVONTE   Psssssssssssst!

          They both turn around. NICOLE *is stunned.*
          SHEVON *is unimpressed.*

SHEVON   Ummmm, I know you're not pssssting me like
          I'm some kinda dog! Pet store? That way. And
          while you're there, go pick up some friggin
          manners, Devonte!
DEVONTE   Yo whatever, I wasn't tryna talk to you
          anyhow.
SHEVON   Man, move from here with your broke ass!
          Ain't no one tryna talk to you!

          They hear a car horn and look around.

DEVONTE   Jeez! Is that a Cadillac CTS?
SHEVON   Yup.
NICOLE   I guess your curfew is up.
SHEVON   He just came to give me a ride home. He's a
          gentleman like that.

NICOLE   Mmmm-hmm.

SHEVON   Hey, I don't judge you.

> *SHEVON looks DEVONTE up and down pointedly.*

DEVONTE   Yo, Shevon, you think you can ask Winston if I could swing by some time and holler at him now that I'm back?

> *SHEVON rolls her eyes.*

SHEVON   Nicole, I'll call you later about this weekend.

> *SHEVON exits.*

DEVONTE   Yo, what's wrong wit your girl?

NICOLE   Shevon's just Shevon.

DEVONTE   Hmph.

> *Pause.*

NICOLE   I better go. I was on my way to the store and—

DEVONTE   Nicole.

NICOLE   What?

DEVONTE   Can you just . . . chill . . . for a second . . .

NICOLE   Fine. But I really can't stay long.

> *They sit awkwardly in silence.*

DEVONTE   Long time.

NICOLE   Yeah. When did you get back?

DEVONTE	I've been back for a coupla months.
NICOLE	Oh.
DEVONTE	Yeah.

Silence.

NICOLE	So how's Alberta?
DEVONTE	Cold as fuck.
NICOLE	You hate the cold.
DEVONTE	Man, it was the worst. Two years in that bitch.

Pause.

	I heard you had a kid.
NICOLE	I did.
DEVONTE	Eight months?
NICOLE	Yup. I guess you did your homework.
DEVONTE	Something like that. Congrats.
NICOLE	Thank you.
DEVONTE	What's he like?
NICOLE	Amazing. A handful. Crawling everywhere, trying to walk. He's super smart. Surprises me every day.
DEVONTE	I'm happy for you.
NICOLE	I named him Zakiya.
DEVONTE	I heard.

They look at each other for a moment, then look away. Both speak at the same time.

	How's work?
NICOLE	How's your mom?

DEVONTE   Sorry.

NICOLE   No. My bad. Work's whatever. Still at
          Shoppers.

DEVONTE   You've been there for a minute, huh?

NICOLE   Yeah.

Silence.

I'm actually thinking about going back to
school.

DEVONTE   Oh yeah? To do what?

NICOLE   I'm not sure yet. I was thinking something like
          psychology.

DEVONTE   Okay, okay.

NICOLE   But then I want to make money so maybe
          business . . .

DEVONTE   I hear that.

NICOLE   Yeah, I just want to wait for Zakiya to get a bit
          bigger, but after that I want to make some real
          moves.

DEVONTE   For sure. That's a good look. I'd come to you
          for some therapy.

NICOLE laughs.

NICOLE   You probably need some therapy.

Silence.

And what about you?

DEVONTE   What about me?

NICOLE   You going back to school?

DEVONTE	Man . . . that shit's a waste of time.
	Look how old I am.
NICOLE	Yeah. So?
DEVONTE	I can't be going back now.
NICOLE	You can do adult school, or summer school—
DEVONTE	Naw, man.

Silence.

| | Besides they're still pulling the same stunts they was when I was a yute—tryna send mans to the VP's office for being late. I ain't got time for none of that . . . |
| NICOLE | So you're just gonna be a dropout then? |

Silence.

	Maybe you just need to switch schools and start fresh somewhere . . .
DEVONTE	It's not that simple . . .
NICOLE	Paulo Coelho says: "There is only one thing that makes a dream impossible to achieve: the fear of failure."
DEVONTE	I almost forgot about you and your quotes. I'm not scared, I just . . . I can't be rolling up in schools in another hood . . . it's complicated. Next subject.

Silence.

| NICOLE | I heard about your moms. |

DEVONTE	Yeah. Thanks for . . . I heard you checked in and—
NICOLE	I just wanted to . . . it's nothing.
DEVONTE	It's not nothing.

Silence.

NICOLE	If you ever want to talk . . .
DEVONTE	I know. Thanks. Oh before I forget.

He quietly sticks a wad of bills in her pocket.

NICOLE	Devonte—
DEVONTE	Nah, man, don't even start.
NICOLE	I'm not a charity case just 'cause I have a baby—
DEVONTE	I'm not saying you are.
NICOLE	I'm working something out . . .
DEVONTE	Yo don't make a big deal out of this.
NICOLE	But—
DEVONTE	Nicole, can you just let me help you? I want to. Just put it towards the groceries or something.
NICOLE	This is way more than groceries.
DEVONTE	Then I dunno, make it a special night and go to Sobeys instead of No Frills or something.

NICOLE laughs.

NICOLE	Thank you.

Pause.

Where'd you get—

NICOLE   Nicole. Don't.

Silence. DEVONTE *is watching* NICOLE.

I'm feeling what you did with your hair.

NICOLE   Whatever.

DEVONTE   Why you whatevering me?

NICOLE   I don't like when people gas me.

DEVONTE   Well I'm not people. And I'm not gassing.

They look at each other.

It's really good to see you.

They keep looking at each other. They are disrupted by the sound of the police. They both stand.

Fuck.

NICOLE   You have?

DEVONTE   Naw.

They stand to face the officer.

OFFICER   ID.

DEVONTE *passes him his ID.*

Well, well. We meet again. You're getting pretty comfortable on this court. Why do I keep finding you here?

DEVONTE	I could ask you the same thing.
OFFICER	All right, smart guy. You know the deal. Hands on the wall.

DEVONTE *raises his hands.*

NICOLE	He didn't do anything.
OFFICER	Miss, stay out of police business.
DEVONTE	Yo, you heard her. I didn't do nothing.
OFFICER	Unlikely.
DEVONTE	Ain't there a law against harassment?
OFFICER	There's no such thing as harassing a criminal.
DEVONTE	Innocent until proven guilty, Officer. Ain't that right? So what's the deal? You arresting me right now? What's the charge, Officer? Yo boss, you having a bad day? You're not even searching me right. Why you actin like this your first time?
OFFICER	Shut it.
DEVONTE	I'm just saying. You're pattin me down mad awkward like you don't know what you're looking for. Just be careful to keep it to pattin and no feely-feely ting. My girl's standing right there and true say mans don't roll that way with no bwoy-dem.
OFFICER	All right, all right. Hands down. What's your business here?
DEVONTE	Well, let's see. I was just here talking to my girl, enjoying the sunshine, watching some ball and then you pulled up. How 'bout you tell us what your business is here?

| OFFICER | Neighbourhood policing. Miss, I have a few questions for you. |

NICOLE reluctantly moves over to the officer.

	Have you witnessed this individual conducting any criminal activity?
NICOLE	No.
OFFICER	Did he ever try to involve you in any criminal activity?
NICOLE	No.
OFFICER	Do you know that if you lie you can be charged as an accomplice?

Silence.

| | Fine. I'm sure I'll be seeing you both again. |
| DEVONTE | Yeah whatever. |

They watch the officer exit. Silence.

| NICOLE | It's so fucked up that they can just do that. I swear we need our own police to protect us from the police, you know? |

Silence.

Devonte? Devonte—

DEVONTE gets up abruptly.

DEVONTE   I got some business I gotta handle. I'll catch
           you later.

>   *DEVONTE exits. NICOLE leans back and lets*
>   *out a long sigh before checking the time on*
>   *her phone, jumping up and exiting.*

SCENE 4

The Movement is hosting a meeting. The space is filled with activists old and young and KHALIL *is addressing an elder.* BEVERLY *is giving out food and drinks to those present.* AKILAH *is taking notes.*

AKILAH   Okay, everyone, let's get some—

KHALIL   *(to* ELDER*)* You're calling us radical? By day teachers are poisoning the minds of our children and by night police are murdering our brothers.

ELDER   I know that.

KHALIL   They could stream Akilah's son Josiah tomorrow. They could murder me tonight. It is not radical to resist when your mind and your life are at stake. It is rational to resist by any means necessary and by all means available.

ELDER   Now just because you read a Malcolm X speech or two does not mean you get to come in here and showboat your way into this meeting with your antics.

KHALIL Antics?

ELDER Yes antics.

KHALIL Wow.

ELDER You're being overly dramatic. Typical of you young people—

AKILAH Please don't patronize us when we—

ELDER Always ready for the short sprint when you need to be training for a marathon.

KHALIL Am I being dramatic or are you being a coward?

ELDER A coward? This coming from the one taking seven years and counting to finish a degree?

KHALIL That's not true and it has nothing to do with—

AKILAH All right I think we should—

ELDER You just think you can disrespect—

KHALIL No disrespect is intended, Elder—

ELDER Now who is patronizing who?

KHALIL —but we have no time for dilly-dallying when our people are dying—

AKILAH This isn't helping—

ELDER Don't tell me about my people—

KHALIL Your people? They're not your people.

ELDER That's not what I meant and you know it. You're just—

KHALIL It is exactly that possessive—

AKILAH Okay, everyone, stop. I didn't beg my aunt to babysit so that I could listen to you two bicker with each other. This isn't accomplishing anything.

ELDER	Well I was trying to accomplish something before this upstart—
AKILAH	Please. I can't—
KHALIL	Akilah. You know what I'm getting at.
AKILAH	I do. I just—
KHALIL	All I'm saying is these meetings aren't enough.
ELDER	I know that.
KHALIL	I'm tired of the intellectual bullshit. It's like Brother Kwame said—we have to move from acknowledging that shit is bad to resisting that bad shit.
ELDER	Please. Brother Kwame? That Disney revolutionary? He isn't even here. Hasn't been here for the past three meetings.

KHALIL and AKILAH glance at each other.

KHALIL	He's got some other pressing business he has to take care of.

KHALIL signals for BEVERLY to get water for him.

ELDER	And resistance? Your resistance is just code for getting people arrested.
KHALIL	My man, you need to understand. We're in a war right now. In the name of our ancestors, in the name of the land we were stolen from, in the name of—
ELDER	Oh lawd . . . here he goes again with his speechifying.

KHALIL   —the decent housing we have no access to, in the name of the education we deserve and in the name of justice, we must tear down this corrupt system and do unto our oppressors as they have done unto us.

ELDER   Okay now hold on. What you are suggesting is retribution!

KHALIL   And?

ELDER   That is not what this meeting was called for.

KHALIL   Are you too scared to take a stand, brother?

ELDER   Too scared? Isn't it convenient how easily you seem to forget what we went through so you can sit here lecturizing? So you're just gonna forget about the sleeping car porters and the domestic workers and the Congress of Black Writers and St. George University where they yelled "let the niggers burn"? You're just gonna dash 'way alla that history of organizing? You may have read Malcolm, but I heard the man speak! Here we are fighting these school systems, trying to get our history in the books, but look at dis. I'm giving the history to you, but you're too busy smelling yourself to realize you've signed up for voluntary amnesia.

Silence.

AKILAH   Okay. Maybe we should take a break and cool down a bit.

AKILAH goes to speak with ELDER while KHALIL turns to BEVERLY. AKILAH notices.

KHALIL   Welcome to the Movement.

BEVERLY   Wow. This is intense . . .

KHALIL   Yeah it can be.

BEVERLY   It's strange though.

KHALIL   What is?

BEVERLY   I mean you've talked a lot about what we're
            reacting to or . . . what we're gonna break
            down but . . . this might be a silly question.
            I just . . . I don't understand . . . what are we
            trying to build? If we don't like how things are
            right now, what's the vision for the alternative?

            Pause.

KHALIL   Hm . . . that's a really interesting—

AKILAH   Beverly, can you get the patties out of the oven
            please?

BEVERLY   Sure.
            (to KHALIL) Sorry what were you about to—

AKILAH   Now. Please.

            *BEVERLY gets up. KHALIL and AKILAH
            exchange looks and then KHALIL drifts off
            thinking.*

SCENE 5

NICOLE is in her apartment, sitting on the ground creating her vision board. DEVONTE knocks on her door. NICOLE answers.

NICOLE   Hi . . .

DEVONTE   Hey!

NICOLE   Ummm . . . is everything good?

DEVONTE   Yeah. I just wanted to check in . . . I hope it's cool . . . I brought Zakiya a little something.

NICOLE   Thomas the Tank Engine! He'll love this. But it's way past his bedtime . . .

DEVONTE   Oh right. Yeah. I guess it is kinda late.

NICOLE   Yeah.

DEVONTE   My bad. I brought you something too.

He opens a plastic bag.

NICOLE   Mmmm. Those patties from Randy's?

DEVONTE   Yup.

NICOLE   You know that's my weakness. Come in.

        DEVONTE enters.

Ummm shoes.

        *DEVONTE backtracks and takes off his shoes.
        He looks around.*

DEVONTE   So this is your spot. Not bad at all.
  NICOLE   Yeah. Ke-ke came through. Housing woulda
            had me on that waiting list forever.
DEVONTE   What's all this?
  NICOLE   You're gonna laugh.
DEVONTE   I would never laugh at you.
  NICOLE   Liar.
DEVONTE   Pinky swear.

        *They pinky swear. It's an elaborate hand-
        shake that ends with their pinkies linked.*

  NICOLE   I'm making a vision board.
DEVONTE   A vision board? What's that?
  NICOLE   It's this thing Iyanla Vanzant—
DEVONTE   Is that that Oprah lady—
  NICOLE   Yeah!
DEVONTE   —who gives the bad advice?
  NICOLE   Wait, what are you talking about? She gives
            good advice!
DEVONTE   Eehhh . . . debatable. So what does the vision
            board do?
  NICOLE   It doesn't really do anything.

DEVONTE	So what's the point?
NICOLE	I guess when you take the goal out of your mind and put it on the board you're making a promise to yourself and the universe or something that you're gonna make sure this thing happens. It's like deciding to affirm something beyond what this moment tells you is possible.

Pause.

DEVONTE	Man I missed you.

They look at each other.

NICOLE	Ummm . . . do you want a drink or something?
DEVONTE	Sure.
NICOLE	Guinness?
DEVONTE	You know it.

NICOLE gets the drink and plates for the patties.

So these are your goals huh? You want to write? And go to school at Howard? And a house. Why's Iverson here?

NICOLE	Uhh . . . don't worry about that.
DEVONTE	You know he ain't six foot. And he can't rap.
NICOLE	You're a hater. Let me just pack this stuff up.
DEVONTE	I'm playing wit you. I'm just curious. About you.
NICOLE	I don't like being exposed.
DEVONTE	I kinda like you exposed.

NICOLE	Okay, let's make this fair. What's on your vision board?
DEVONTE	I don't have a vision board.
NICOLE	Just say you did. What's one thing you want to accomplish in life or one dream that you have for yourself.
DEVONTE	I don't know. Make money?
NICOLE	That's original. What else?

DEVONTE shrugs.

	You don't have no dreams? Nothing you want to do?
DEVONTE	Yeah but . . .
NICOLE	But what?
DEVONTE	It's just too late.
NICOLE	Says who?
DEVONTE	Doesn't matter.
NICOLE	Yeah it does matter. If you make this about other people you'll always have an excuse. It's about you.
DEVONTE	When did you get so smart?
NICOLE	I was always so smart. You were just too slow to realize.

DEVONTE chuckles.

	Can I ask you something?
DEVONTE	Yeah.
NICOLE	Remember when the po-po rolled up at the court last week?
DEVONTE	Yeah.

NICOLE	You called me your girl.
DEVONTE	No I didn't.
NICOLE	Yeah you did. You said, "I'm just here, talking to my girl."
DEVONTE	For real? Okay maybe I did. What's the question?

Silence.

You want to know if you're really my girl?

Pause.

Nicole. In my mind, you never stopped being my girl.

NICOLE	You just left.
DEVONTE	I know . . . it was complicated.
NICOLE	You know it's not like before Devonte. I have another person with me.
DEVONTE	I know.
NICOLE	And you're okay with that?
DEVONTE	I mean it's not ideal but it is what it is.
NICOLE	What does that mean?
DEVONTE	Imma show you what that means.

They look at each other and move closer together, standing so close their noses almost touch. Zakiya starts crying.

NICOLE	Sorry.
DEVONTE	It's cool.
NICOLE	I'll be right back.

NICOLE exits. DEVONTE's phone rings. He answers.

DEVONTE   Yeah?

He checks to see if NICOLE has come back and moves away from Zakiya's room.

Yo. I can't talk right now . . . I just said now's not a good time . . . I'll link you later . . . yeah. All right. One.

NICOLE enters.

NICOLE   You good?

DEVONTE   I'm great. So you gonna help me make my first vision board or? . . .

They smile at each other.

SCENE 6

*It is 1970-something and we are back at
the meeting being held by the Movement.
Throughout the meeting* KHALIL *glances
at* BEVERLY *and exchanges a smile or two.*
AKILAH *notices and is visibly uncomfortable.*
BEVERLY *is taking notes.*

KHALIL   What we need to do is start building a vision
        for the future.

ELDER   What does that mean?

KHALIL   We need to stop reacting and begin building.

ELDER   Who invited the poet?

AKILAH   Okay. Elder, what do you think we should do?

ELDER   We should be focusing our efforts on lobbying.

Everyone groans.

	We have to reform the system. We can't spiral out of control, rioting and mashing up the place. We need to rein the people them back in.
KHALIL	Why? There is a rise in Black militancy. Black people aren't begging—
ELDER	Black militancy? What are you trying to do? Build an army? Start shooting at the pigs?
KHALIL	People have a right to be angry.
ELDER	I'm not saying that they don't but—
AKILAH	My son is eight years old and I can see teachers trying to devalue his worth every day. I can see him confused and angry. Josiah has a right to be angry.
ELDER	So what—you want to teach Josiah to riot?
AKILAH	No. I am going to teach Josiah how to channel his anger, know the power of his voice. I want him to be able to stand up and defend himself when a teacher—
ELDER	How touching. Listen, young lady, there is a distinct difference between holding up a placard at Christie Pits and organizing a community.
AKILAH	My name is not young lady.
ELDER	Oh lawd. Here we go. Okay. Okay, Akee-wah. Calm down.
AKILAH	It's Akilah.
ELDER	Aren't you supposed to be taking the minutes?

Silence.

| BEVERLY | I think . . . if I may . . . I think that the problem is we don't know how powerful we are. |

ELDER	Who are you? Who is she?
BEVERLY	I'm Beverly. Hi. I'm new. I just . . . I think that . . . I mean I'm not an expert but I don't think that you can expect society to change if you're not ready to take the first step.
ELDER	The first step? My girl, I've taken the first, second, third and fourth steps! Do you know how long I've been doing this?
BEVERLY	I . . . I just think that if we're building a real Black political movement then we have to make sure that . . .
ELDER	That what?
BEVERLY	I don't know . . . nothing. Sorry.
AKILAH	Don't apologize.
BEVERLY	What?
AKILAH	Speak up.
BEVERLY	Well I just think that people have to start thinking about what resistance means on an individual level—like personally.
KHALIL	I think I get what the sister is saying. So for example, one step someone might want to take is getting the white out of their hair.

ELDER self-consciously touches his hair.

BEVERLY	That's not exactly what I—
KHALIL	A second step could be getting the white out of their mind.
ELDER	Are you insinuating that—?
AKILAH	Ahhh I think I know where you're going with this, brother. Maybe a third step could be . . .

for a few people in this meeting . . . getting the white woman out of their bedroom.

ELDER and KHALIL react at the same time.

ELDER   Hol on! Hol on!

KHALIL   Whoa!

ELDER   Now we don't have to start going into people's private affairs—

KHALIL   I don't think that's pertinent to the conversation—

ELDER   I say we take another break.

KHALIL   I agree. Yes, a break is good.

AKILAH   Look at that. You've finally found something you both can agree on.

SCENE 7

DEVONTE *approaches hesitantly. He is at the guidance counsellor's office at school.*

MS. FLYNN Can I help you?

DEVONTE Yeah, I wanted to—

MS. FLYNN Young man, we can't begin until you take off your hat.

DEVONTE *takes off his hat.*

DEVONTE I wanted to know if—

A phone rings.

MS. FLYNN Hold on one moment— Hello, Mirror Collegiate, Guidance Office, Melinda Flynn speaking. Mmm-hhhmmm. Okay. No. That is incorrect. You need to get the green form. Yes. The blue one is for the grade nines. Yes. No, they're not on the website. You'll have to come by the school. Yes. Okay then. No problem. Goodbye.

She hangs up the phone.

Go on.

DEVONTE   I just wanted to know if it would be possible for me to, like, or how I could start working on a plan to . . . okay, sorry. Let me start over. Basically I'm missing a couple of credits.

MS. FLYNN   Mmm-hmm.

DEVONTE   But I want to go to university.

MS. FLYNN   Really?

DEVONTE   Yeah.

MS. FLYNN   You want to go to university?

DEVONTE   Yeah.

MS. FLYNN   And study what?

DEVONTE   I'm not sure yet.

MS. FLYNN   You don't know what you want to study?

DEVONTE   Nah but I just want to try and get there.

MS. FLYNN   Hmm.

DEVONTE   So . . . I was just wondering how I could do that, like if you could help me make a plan towards that or something.

MS. FLYNN   Devonte . . . Ellis right?

DEVONTE   Yeah.

She types on the computer, looks at the screen, looks at DEVONTE and then back to the screen.

MS. FLYNN	Hmm. It looks like you're missing more than a couple of credits. You don't have any of your grade eleven courses completed.
DEVONTE	Yeah I was away during that time.
MS. FLYNN	Away?
DEVONTE	Yeah . . . But I saw this flyer in the community centre about these transitional programs or something for people like me who get off track.
MS. FLYNN	Okay.
DEVONTE	So I wanted to sign up for one.

MS. FLYNN sighs.

MS. FLYNN	Have you thought about this, Devonte?
DEVONTE	Yeah. That's why I'm here.
MS. FLYNN	I mean have you really sat down and thought this through? These transitional programs are for people who have demonstrated potential. It's not just for people who have gone off track. You have to demonstrate that you could succeed in them.
DEVONTE	Okay, so that's why I'm asking how do I do that?
MS. FLYNN	These programs are a lot of work and require a tremendous amount of discipline. I'm scanning your record and alongside your grades you've been late an astonishing number of times, Devonte, not to mention your absences. You can't be late like that in these programs.
DEVONTE	Okay, so I won't be late anymore. I'll come to school every day. Just tell me what else I gotta do.

MS. FLYNN sighs.

MS. FLYNN   I just . . . I don't know if this is the right plan
for you. I don't know if it is a realistic one.
It might be better just to sign up for a GED
program and get your diploma and then—hear
me out—look into a trade. You can get a lot
of good money in the trades and make a good,
honest living. Have you thought about something like that?

DEVONTE   I don't want to do a trade.

MS. FLYNN   Here. Take a look at these pamphlets. They
describe the GED program and all the various
things you can do. There is a lot of opportunity and I just . . . I think with your record as it
stands . . . this might be a more realistic option
for you. Maybe you don't do a trade but there
are other things available with a GED. And
then come back and see me. Sound like a plan?

DEVONTE   Yeah.

The phone rings.

MS. FLYNN   Hello, Mirror Collegiate, Guidance Office,
Melinda Flynn speaking.

*DEVONTE begins to leave, hesitates and then
puts on his hat and exits.*

SCENE 8

*NICOLE is walking with a stroller. She stops
at various points to make her inquiries.*

NICOLE   Hi. I'm looking for daycare for my son.

WORKER 1   Well you've come to the right place. What's
his name?

NICOLE   This is Zakiya.

WORKER 1   Hello, Zakiya! Look at those bright eyes!

NICOLE   I heard about this place on *Breakfast
Television.*

WORKER 1   Oh wonderful!

NICOLE   They were saying a lot of good things about
you guys.

WORKER 1   Thank you. We believe that in order to provide
quality care, you need quality staff. Our staff-
to-child ratio is one to four.

NICOLE   That's so good.

WORKER 1   Yes. For our toddlers we provide instruction in
French, computers and mathematics.

NICOLE   Wow. You hear that, Zakiya. You're gonna be speaking French!

WORKER 1   Babies are the fastest learners. But we also believe in the power of play. We have a yard in the back for the kids to play in and in the spring we do a little gardening too.

NICOLE   Wow. That all sounds amazing. This is exactly the kind of place I want my son to be. I just want him to be exposed to a lot of the things I didn't get, you know?

WORKER 1   Of course! That's the hope of every good mother.

NICOLE   So umm . . . the *Breakfast Television* thing didn't say how much it cost.

WORKER 1   We charge $2,075.

NICOLE   A year?

WORKER 1   No. A month.

NICOLE   A month? Right. A month. Of course. Great. Thanks for the info. I'll definitely take this place into consideration. Thanks.

NICOLE pushes the stroller to another daycare.

Hi, I'm looking for daycare for my son.

WORKER 2   How old is he?

NICOLE   Eight months.

WORKER 2   Sorry, we don't go that young.

NICOLE pushes the stroller to a daycare.

NICOLE	Excuse me? Hi. You guys have daycare for infants, right?
WORKER 3	Yes we do, but we're completely full right now.
NICOLE	Crap. Like full full?
WORKER 3	Yes. Full full. I can put you on a waiting list though.
NICOLE	Okay. How long is the waiting list?
WORKER 3	There are currently 163 children on the list.

NICOLE sighs and pushes her stroller to another daycare.

NICOLE	Do you have any room in your daycare?
WORKER 4	Yeah I have room.
NICOLE	How much do you charge a month?
WORKER 4	Three hundred dollars a week.
NICOLE	Okay.
WORKER 4	Plus a non-refundable registration fee of seventy-five dollars.
NICOLE	Okay.
WORKER 4	And I don't do diapers.
NICOLE	What do you mean?
WORKER 4	I don't change diapers. If your baby needs his diaper changed, I call you.
NICOLE	But I'll be at work.
WORKER 4	So then you'll change it after.
NICOLE	What kind of bullshit . . .

NICOLE pushes her stroller away, pulls out her cellphone and makes a call.

Hey, Tracy, can you take my shift tomorrow? I know . . . I'm sorry to ask again but I need another day. I can't find anyone to watch Zakiya. Please. I'll owe you. Thank you.

NICOLE *hangs up. She sighs and walks off with the stroller.*

SCENE 9

*We are in the office of the Movement with
ELDER, KHALIL and AKILAH. AKILAH is standing between the two desks where ELDER and
KHALIL are seated. She carries a tired energy
about her.*

KHALIL Akilah, given the new threats that have been
made on the protest did you talk to Brother
Kwame about the defensive strategy?

AKILAH We're meeting on Tuesday. There wasn't
enough time to—

ELDER Sister Akeee-wah—

AKILAH Akee-LAH.

ELDER Yes, yes. Have you briefed the new volunteers
on the security protocol?

AKILAH Yes, I began doing that—

KHALIL What about the lesson plans for the Liberation
School this week?

AKILAH Yes, I have them ready, I just have to—

ELDER	Sister Akilah, were you able to pick up the supplies for the clinic?
AKILAH	*(to ELDER)* No, I was gonna do that right after—
KHALIL	Akilah we need you to facilitate a workshop tomorrow.
AKILAH	*(to KHALIL)* Uhhh okay . . . I'll need child care. Can someone watch my son for the afternoon?

Silence as KHALIL and ELDER avoid her eye contact and keep working.

Forget it. I'll figure it out.

BEVERLY enters.

BEVERLY	Guess what?
AKILAH	What?
BEVERLY	Brother Khalil asked me to write a speech for the march!
AKILAH	*(to BEVERLY)* He did?
KHALIL	I did.
BEVERLY	I think he's warming up to me!
AKILAH	*(suspiciously)* He is?
KHALIL	I am.
BEVERLY	*(to AKILAH)* Could you look over a draft?
AKILAH	Of what?
BEVERLY	Of my speech.
AKILAH	Sure, I just need to find a babysitter . . .
KHALIL	Can you make edits on the press release for tomorrow morning?
AKILAH	Yes, I can.

ELDER	Akilah, your son is on the phone.
AKILAH	I'll be right there!
ELDER	Akilah, we need you in this meeting.
AKILAH	Yes, I'm coming.
KHALIL	Akilah! The meeting has started.
AKILAH	Yes, just give me a second!
ELDER	Akilah can you take the minutes?
AKILAH	Yes, I will, yes I am . . . yes, yes, yes!
BEVERLY	Akilah? Akilah?
AKILAH	What?
BEVERLY	Are you okay?
AKILAH	I don't know. I feel like—
KHALIL	Of course she's okay. Sister Akilah is a strong Black woman who knows that nothing is more important than the revolutionary cause. Sister Akilah is a soldier who brings the people out of the destructive reactionary petty bourgeoisie jive slave mentality and cleanses them of their brainwashing through re-education. Sister Akilah is the kind of woman who can birth the baby while washing the clothes and cooking the food and training the comrades and cleaning the office and raising the funds and packing the groceries. Sister Akilah can do it all. Sister Akilah—
AKILAH	Is tired.
BEVERLY	What did you say?
AKILAH	Nothing.
BEVERLY	You said you were tired. Didn't you?
ELDER	Tired?

ELDER kisses his teeth.

KHALIL & ELDER	There is no room in the revolution for tired.

KHALIL and ELDER *exit.*

AKILAH	It's true. You'll learn that soon enough.
BEVERLY	You can't do it all.
AKILAH	Watch me.
BEVERLY	Maybe . . . you should rest.
AKILAH	What?
BEVERLY	It just . . . it seems like you're working really hard.
AKILAH	Everyone is working hard.
BEVERLY	Yeah but you work really, really hard.
AKILAH	I know I do. I don't need you to tell me that.
BEVERLY	I'm just saying that maybe you need a break or something . . .
AKILAH	There is no time for—I don't know why I'm explaining myself to you. You have no idea how much we need to do.
BEVERLY	Okay but—
AKILAH	You're just a floater. You float from city to city. It's easy for you to have an opinion because you don't stay in one place long enough to use that opinion in any way that will make a difference.
BEVERLY	I'm just trying to help.
AKILAH	Who said I need help? And if I did, it wouldn't be from someone so naive.
BEVERLY	I'm not naive.
AKILAH	Please. Why do you think Khalil asked you to write that speech for the march?
BEVERLY	What? What do you mean?

AKILAH   Like I said. I don't need help from someone so
         naive.

         They sit in silence.

         Why are you still here? Just go.

         BEVERLY *begins to leave and then stops and*
         returns. AKILAH *sighs.*

         I don't know when it stopped being . . .
BEVERLY What?
AKILAH   I don't know what the word is. Hopeful?
         Energizing? Beautiful, I guess. I don't remem-
         ber when it stopped being beautiful. There
         were a few good years . . . really good years. I
         used to write a lot. I even organized a poetry
         collective.
BEVERLY You did?
AKILAH   I did. Man, you should have seen how packed
         the spot would get. I fell in love.
BEVERLY Falling in love is beautiful.
AKILAH   Yeah. I just believed, I really believed that we
         could do this. We could do this freedom thing
         through art and passion and . . .
BEVERLY . . . and then what happened?
AKILAH   And then reality. My son was born and
         the stakes were raised and I was suddenly
         alone, in charge of this little life . . . and
         then Kathleen fled the country and Kennedy
         fled the country and Stokely fled the coun-
         try and LeRoi was arrested and Angela was

arrested and Assata was arrested and Afeni was arrested and Leonard was arrested and Rap was arrested and Huey was arrested and Rosie was arrested and Anne was arrested and Lumumba was killed and Medgar was killed and Malcolm was killed and King was killed and Jonathan was killed and Fred was killed and George was killed . . . and I was still here . . . with my words all dried up. I guess that was around the time it stopped being beautiful.

BEVERLY Damn.

AKILAH Yeah. Anyway. It doesn't matter. There's work to do and it has to get done. Ten, twenty years from now, Josiah can't be sitting in meetings still talking about racist school systems and trigger-happy police.

BEVERLY Yeah but . . . what about the love?

Silence.

What about the passion? The art? You still need those things. Your son needs to know about those things too, right?

AKILAH My son needs to live. That's what he needs to do. He needs to be alive. He needs to not be on the run or live in a jail cell. You just got here. You have no idea what this thing is.

BEVERLY I might not know the difference between a Trotskyite and a Leninist but I do know that I want to do more than survive. You've been through a lot and . . . grieving takes time.

You can't live on anger—you can't build on it.
It's . . . stupid. You need love. You really do.

*AKILAH struggles to remain composed. They
sit in silence.*

I'm only part-time at the bookstore. I could
look after Josiah sometimes . . . if you want.

*After a moment, AKILAH nods without
looking at her. The phone rings and AKILAH
picks up.*

AKILAH   Hello. Yes it is . . . I see . . . When? . . .
Where? . . . What's the charge? . . . Why
not? . . . Okay so is there a charge? . . . Got it.

She hangs up.

BEVERLY   What happened?
AKILAH   Khalil's been arrested.
BEVERLY   What?
AKILAH   I have to go. Call the lawyer and have them
meet me at 13th Division.
BEVERLY   But—

*AKILAH exits while BEVERLY sits stunned
before picking up the phone.*

SCENE 10

SHEVON and NICOLE *are sitting on a couch
at* NICOLE's *apartment while* NICOLE *packs a
baby bag for Zakiya.* SHEVON *is only half lis-
tening to* NICOLE *and is clearly distracted.*

NICOLE   So I'm on hold with Toronto Children's
Services for like forty-five minutes, only to
be told that I'm gonna be put on a waiting
list and there are eighteen thousand children
ahead of mine. Eighteen thousand! By the time
they get to Zakiya he'll be graduating fucking
high school. Like what's the point of saying
you have a subsidy if barely anyone can get it?
This whole system is backwards. There has to
be another way. Like back in the day, it didn't
seem like people were relying on daycare. You
found your tribe and got support and stuff.
Everything just feels so broken now you know?
Hello? Shevon?

SHEVON	Oh. Yeah. Man fuck the police.
NICOLE	What? Yo, what is up with you? You've been acting haunted since you walked through the door.
SHEVON	Do you think there was ever a time when men gave women the respect they deserve?
NICOLE	Probably not. Why?
SHEVON	He's cheating on me.
NICOLE	How do you know?
SHEVON	I just know.
NICOLE	That's not an answer.
SHEVON	Trust me on this.
NICOLE	You come with this drama every month.
SHEVON	This time is different.
NICOLE	Why?
SHEVON	It just is.
NICOLE	Did you see a text? Did you sneak into his Myspace? Did you follow him?
SHEVON	I've got chlamydia.
NICOLE	What?!
SHEVON	I went to the clinic this morning. This mother-fucka gave me chlamydia.
NICOLE	Holy shit.

Silence.

SHEVON	You must think I'm an idiot.
NICOLE	I don't think you're an idiot.
SHEVON	I should have seen this man was a waste yute.
NICOLE	He wasn't waste in the beginning.
SHEVON	He wasn't, right?

*WINSTON enters with a distinctive swagger
and approaches SHEVON, taking her hand as
she relives the memory.*

WINSTON   Yo, boom. You're the one I want, seen? Forget
dem hos. I'm not even preein them. You're the
wifey, seen?

They walk around hand in hand.

So tell me. Where you want to go shopping?

SHEVON   You're taking me shopping?

WINSTON   Of course! Anywhere you want.

SHEVON   Shopping for what?

WINSTON   Any ting you want!

SHEVON   Hmmm . . . how about Yorkdale Mall?

WINSTON   Yorkdale? Yorkdale? Bun' a Yorkdale and
they're ragga-ragga shops! I'm taking you to
Yorkville! My woman only wears the toppa top
tings, you feel me?

*SHEVON begins modelling outfits as though in
front of a mirror.*

Mmm-hmmm! Now that's what I'm talking
'bout. Turn around? Damn. My baby is fine.
You want one in every colour? Any ting you
want, boo.

*SHEVON speaks to NICOLE but looks at
WINSTON while speaking.*

SHEVON	I know mad girls were hating 'cause he chose me. And I loved it.
WINSTON	Baby girl, you know is me and you, seen? No one else matters. Me and you against the world.
NICOLE	I remember.
SHEVON	It didn't stay like that. All of a sudden he went from buying my clothes to picking out my clothes.
WINSTON	You want to wear what? Nah. Change dat. Put dis on! My wifey's not walking on road looking like some slu ting.
SHEVON	Then came the interrogations.
WINSTON	Where were you today?
SHEVON	At Nicole's.
WINSTON	Yeah? You were at Nicole's house all day?
SHEVON	Yeah.
WINSTON	All day you were at Nicole's house?
SHEVON	Yeah.
WINSTON	You never left Nicole's house?
SHEVON	Ummm . . .
WINSTON	Umm what?
SHEVON	Okay you remember my friend Joel with the buckteeth? His mom is really sick and I went to go see him to drop off a card. I was only there for five minutes, I swear, and then I went to Nicole's.
WINSTON	Yeah, eh? What time was that?
SHEVON	I'm not sure . . .
WINSTON	About 3:30 you think?
SHEVON	I don't know.
WINSTON	Yeah I would say it was around 3:30 because that was the time I called you and that was the

	time you didn't answer. Yeah 3:30 seems about right because that was the time Tuffa told me he saw you go into Joel's building. And he said you came out around four. That sounds like longer than five minutes to me.
SHEVON	I'm sorry.
WINSTON	How many times I gotta tell you? The streets are watching, and I run these streets. You can't hide nuttin from me.
SHEVON	*(to NICOLE)* And then I started working for him.
WINSTON	Shevon, I need you to drop this stuff over at Kareem's by five. If anyone stops you, say you're going to check your uncle, seen?
SHEVON	*(to WINSTON)* Okay. What is it?
WINSTON	Don't concern yourself with none of that. Just drop it off. Seen?
NICOLE	Why didn't you tell me how bad it was?
SHEVON	*(to NICOLE)* Because I knew what you'd say. And you were too busy with Zakiya. Anyway, at first it wasn't a big deal. It started with small favours but they just kept getting bigger.
WINSTON	Hey, Shevon, you know Chris, right?
SHEVON	Which Chris?
WINSTON	The one that stays by Trimbee and plays ball sometimes at the centre.
SHEVON	Oh yeah. I've known him since elementary.
WINSTON	You been to his crib?
SHEVON	Yeah back in the day when he used to have those barbecues.
WINSTON	You been inside?
SHEVON	Yeah.

WINSTON	I need you to draw the layout to his house.
SHEVON	Why?
WINSTON	Don't worry about why.
SHEVON	You're gonna set up Chris?
WINSTON	What did I just say about asking questions?
NICOLE	Is that how Chris ended up in the hospital?
SHEVON	*(to NICOLE)* Yeah.
NICOLE	Damn, Shevon.
SHEVON	I knew it was bad. I knew. But I still did it.
NICOLE	Why?
WINSTON	Because. I said so.

> *SHEVON is pulled between the real-life conversation with NICOLE and the voice of WINSTON in her head. WINSTON is sitting in a corner rolling a spliff, watching her and NICOLE and chiming in every now and then. NICOLE is not able to see or hear him.*

NICOLE	Man fuck Winston. Watch when I see him. This man has done nothing for your life but bring you stress and drama.
WINSTON	You better not bring your homegirls around me with all their stress and drama.
NICOLE	How many times have you had to bail him out of jail?
WINSTON	How many times have I had to tell you don't chat my business?
SHEVON	*(to WINSTON)* But . . .
NICOLE	But nothing. And I don't care what you say, that massive ass tattoo of his name on your neck was a mistake—

SHEVON	*(to NICOLE)* Leave it alone, Nicole.
NICOLE	You couldn't even get Winston? You had to go get Killa? His a.k.a.?
WINSTON	Dun kno.
SHEVON	*(to NICOLE)* It's done . . .
WINSTON	Done? You don't get to decide when this is done.
SHEVON	*(to WINSTON)* No, I was just . . .
NICOLE	You just what? Let him bring drugs up into your parents' house and have custies coming in and out? No respect. And now this?
SHEVON	*(to NICOLE)* I know. I know.
WINSTON	You don't know nothing.
SHEVON	Fuck off!
NICOLE	What?
SHEVON	No, not you—
WINSTON	I'll let you know what you need to know.
SHEVON	Shut up!
NICOLE	Shevon?

Pause.

	Shevon.
SHEVON	I know what I'm gonna do. Can you get your granny's car?
NICOLE	Maybe. Why?
SHEVON	*(to NICOLE)* We vaselining up.
WINSTON	Okaaaay! So that's how you're moving?
SHEVON	Yeah nigga, that's how I'm moving.

> *WINSTON laughs to himself and strolls off stage.*

	First we're gonna go pay a little visit to that dutty ho in Galloway I know he was bonin and probably gave him this nastiness, and then imma buy a shitload of kerosene and we lightin all his gear up. Fuck it, we lightin up his house! Then we'll see what's burning around here!
NICOLE	Okay, Shevy, take a breath.
SHEVON	He can't just get a bligh when he gave me a STI.
NICOLE	Okay, just hold on. Paulo Coelho always says, "Life always waits for some crisis to . . . "
SHEVON	Please spare me the fucking quotes right now, Nicole.
NICOLE	Fine. I'm just saying take a moment to think first.
SHEVON	I'm thinking . . . I want to light his shit on fire!
NICOLE	I get why you're mad. But—
SHEVON	But what, Nicole?
NICOLE	I'm not tryna get locked up.
SHEVON	Are you serious?
NICOLE	I have a son now. I'm trying to get him daycare.
SHEVON	Just get Miss Irene down the hall to watch him.
NICOLE	So he can be dumped in front of a TV screen all day and come home smelling like weed?
SHEVON	It's medicinal!
NICOLE	Whatever. I'm just saying. I gotta go to work. I got plans. Life is different now.
SHEVON	Oh okay. I see how it is.
NICOLE	Shevy. There has to be a plan B.
SHEVON	Okay. Tell me. What does "plan B" look like? Call the police? And tell them what? Umm

excuse me, Officer, my gun-dealing, drug-pushing boyfriend cheated on me and gave me a STI. Can you arrest him please and charge him with being a dirty-ass piece of shit? Or maybe I should turn into Mother Teresa and just sit back, forgive him for his sins, forgive him for disrespecting me, disrespecting my body like it's nothing.

Pause.

Those aren't choices, Nicole.

NICOLE   I know.

SHEVON   I thought you were my homegirl.

NICOLE   I am. I just . . .

SHEVON   I can't do this by myself.

Pause.

NICOLE   You don't have to. I got you.

NICOLE's *phone rings.*

Hello? Yeah. What? When? Fuck. What happened? You know what, forget it . . . just . . . when's the hearing? Okay. Thanks.

She hangs up.

SHEVON   What happened?

NICOLE   Devonte was arrested.

SCENE 11

NICOLE and BEVERLY are back in the visitors'
waiting room of the Don Jail. The scene
opens with a scream of frustration from all
of the visitors before they begin their wait
and sentence of gestures.

GUARD   Numbers three, nine, seventeen, twenty-four
and six.

As each number is called the company lean
forward, demonstrating a desperate hope
and then heave a sigh of disappointment
when their number isn't called. The people
waiting perform a sentence of gestures.
NICOLE and BEVERLY progressively become
more grotesque in their movements. A con-
siderable amount of time passes before the
guard speaks again.

Numbers twenty, thirty-two, forty, eleven and twenty-five.

Everyone continues waiting.

SCENE 12

BEVERLY is working on the typewriter at the office for the Movement. She doesn't notice KHALIL come in at first.

BEVERLY   Khalil! I heard you got out! It's so good to see you!

He walks over to the window and peers out the edge, trying not to be seen.

Uhhh . . . is everything okay?

He doesn't respond but begins pacing, looking agitated.

Akilah said they didn't press charges . . . Khalil?

KHALIL   I need you to close the blinds.

BEVERLY gets up to close the blinds.

BEVERLY What's going on?

KHALIL Two men . . . they've been following me since this morning. Look, over there.

BEVERLY Where?

KHALIL You see that man sitting on the bench.

BEVERLY No.

KHALIL Right there! That's one of them.

BEVERLY We better call Kwame.

She goes to pick up the phone.

KHALIL No.

BEVERLY I think we should, Khalil. You need some protection.

KHALIL I said no! Beverly, put down the phone!

BEVERLY Why?

KHALIL I have a feeling it's been bugged . . . there were some strange clicks I heard in the dial tone when I went to make a call this morning . . .

BEVERLY Really?

KHALIL Yeah. Besides . . . Kwame's been acting funny the past few weeks.

BEVERLY Kwame? Are you serious?

KHALIL Yes I'm serious. I think they got to him.

BEVERLY But he was part of the Black Panther Party.

KHALIL He could be a spy.

BEVERLY But . . . he's contributed so much to the Movement.

KHALIL It doesn't matter.

BEVERLY	He provided the connections to our weapons . . .
KHALIL	Yeah. Did you ever stop to wonder where all those guns came from?
BEVERLY	No. Since when did you start having these suspicions?
KHALIL	Since now! Shit woman. Why you interrogating me? I said don't call Kwame so don't put your hand on the goddamned phone!

Silence. KHALIL begins to pace up and down before speaking again.

	Listen. It hurts me too. Brother Kwame was like a mentor for me.
BEVERLY	I'm sorry.
KHALIL	You have to understand, the pressure is high right now. I'm just trying to keep this thing together and it feels like we're getting attacked everywhere. Cats are acting shifty and I don't know who to trust. The pigs are getting to everyone.
BEVERLY	I understand.

KHALIL looks out the window.

KHALIL	No you don't. He's still there. Damn these pigs. You got any smokes?
BEVERLY	I've got some reefer?
KHALIL	That'll do.

BEVERLY starts rolling.

Ahhh, man. I just remembered I've got a paper due tomorrow.

BEVERLY   Yeah, I have an exam. It's kinda hard balancing everything.

KHALIL   That's an understatement.

BEVERLY   How do you do it? School, the meetings, the articles, the organizing . . .

KHALIL   Don't forget jail. I don't know, you just . . . do it. There's no room in the revolution for tired.

BEVERLY   So I keep hearing. But everyone seems so tired.

KHALIL   Between you and me . . . I'm exhausted. What exam do you have tomorrow?

BEVERLY   Citizenship, Revolution and Society in the 19th Century.

KHALIL   With Lafond?

BEVERLY   Yeah.

KHALIL   In the essay questions, make sure to reference the contemporary Québécois struggle. He loves that.

BEVERLY   Thanks. That's really helpful.

KHALIL looks out the window again.

KHALIL   That guy is still sitting out there. We should mobilize the vanguard.

BEVERLY   Okay. I can begin calling people.

KHALIL   I just told you the telephone is bugged! Don't you listen?

BEVERLY   Right. Sorry.

KHALIL   Just give me a minute. I'll think of something.

He sighs deeply.

	Do you want a drink?
BEVERLY	Sure.
KHALIL	I always keep a little Scotch in here. Don't tell Akilah.
BEVERLY	I won't.
KHALIL	Beverly, I'm . . . I'm sorry if I've been hard on you. It's not personal. You get that, right?
BEVERLY	I think so. There's a lot against us. It makes sense to be cautious.
KHALIL	Exactly. But you've been working hard. Helping with the march, volunteering with the programs. You have great ideas. It's why I put you down to give the speech. I want you to know, I see you.
BEVERLY	Thank you. That means a lot.
KHALIL	We just gotta hope that this isn't all for nothing.
BEVERLY	What do you mean?
KHALIL	I don't know. I just have this feeling . . . we might do all this work, organize these marches, hold these conferences, write these articles and . . . none of it will mean anything. It'll be forgotten.
BEVERLY	Is that what you're scared of? Being forgotten?
KHALIL	Black people get forgotten quite easily . . . just check any history textbook.
BEVERLY	Look at everything you're doing. For the Movement, for our people. The way you fight for us. People look up to you. You're not gonna be forgotten.
KHALIL	You think so?
BEVERLY	I know so.

KHALIL   Thank you, Beverly.

*He looks at her for a moment and then
moves in to kiss her and she moves away.*

BEVERLY   Khalil, I didn't mean—
KHALIL   It's fine.

KHALIL gets up and goes to the window.

BEVERLY   I'm sorry. I wasn't trying to—
KHALIL   I said it's fine.
BEVERLY   Okay but—
KHALIL   Don't you have some work to do?

*KHALIL sits at a desk and pretends to read
and BEVERLY shuffles paper on the desk.
They both move stiffly, avoiding eye contact.
After a while he gets up and looks out the
window again.*

SCENE 13

*NICOLE is outside of a Toronto courthouse
waiting. She is exhausted. She takes a few
deep breaths but it doesn't seem to make
a difference. DEVONTE enters and walks
directly to NICOLE. He moves to hug her.
NICOLE doesn't reciprocate.*

DEVONTE   Man, Nicole, thanks for coming through. I owe
you. You were amazing on that stand. That
lawyer wasn't expecting alla that.

NICOLE   Well I've had some practise.

DEVONTE   Yeah. I appreciate you doing this for me. Again.
And you already know I got you on that bail
money.

Silence.

Were you able to bring any of the stuff I
asked for?

Silence.

What's wrong?

NICOLE   Do you know how much time this took?

DEVONTE   I know.

NICOLE   Do you? Really? You know how much time it
took to find a lawyer who wasn't moving side-
ways? You know how much time it took to go
to the bank and get the money to pay her? You
know how much time it took to call this person
and that person and beg them to write letters of
reference for you? Not to mention collecting the
letters and then taking off work to come here
not once, not twice but three times because
they keep delaying the hearing and—

DEVONTE   Nicole, I know, I know. I'm sorry. It's not
gonna happen again. I promise.

NICOLE   I'm not Shevon.

DEVONTE   I know you're not Shevon.

NICOLE   And I'm not my mom.

DEVONTE   Nicole.

NICOLE   Don't use me.

DEVONTE   Use you?

He looks around and checks his volume.

That's really what you think I'm doing?

NICOLE   I don't know.

Silence.

DEVONTE   Where's Zakiya?

NICOLE	I left him with Miss Irene.
DEVONTE	I thought you didn't want to leave him there?
NICOLE	Well I didn't have much choice.

Silence.

	I tried to come visit you last week.
DEVONTE	Oh yeah?
NICOLE	Yeah. They said you were out of visits.
DEVONTE	Oh that's weird.
NICOLE	Yeah it is weird.
DEVONTE	Yo, let's get outta here.
NICOLE	Do you like jail or something? Are you just trying to get back in?
DEVONTE	Of course not.
NICOLE	Well I don't know. You're constantly just in and out.

Silence.

DEVONTE	Nicole. I tried to do different. I really did. But no one wants to hire a nigga with a rap sheet . . . no one wants to give me a chance so . . .
NICOLE	So . . . what? It's back to the game? Because that always works out so well, right?

Silence.

	We've both seen this movie a million times.
DEVONTE	Well maybe I'm making a different movie.

NICOLE	Are you even saving any of the money you make?
DEVONTE	Under my mattress.
NICOLE	That's not funny.
DEVONTE	What do you want me to say? You want me to go make a vision board? Put up a picture of me with a degree? You want me to get a picket sign and start a protest 'cause no one will hire me?
NICOLE	Maybe! I don't know. I just . . . I know I don't want to be here.
DEVONTE	I understand that but what do you want me to do? I'm doing what I know. I don't know how to do different. I ain't never seen how to do that before.
NICOLE	That's not good enough.
DEVONTE	Well that's all I got. Mans on the block were the ones that checked for me.
NICOLE	Yeah, yeah, yeah. And they took you under their wing and taught you what it is . . . ray ray ray. I'm tired of that story. You think I saw anything different? It doesn't mean I'm willing to accept this as the be all and end all of life.
DEVONTE	Oh so what, you want me to work at ghetto-ass Shoppers like you?

Silence.

	I didn't mean it like that.
NICOLE	I have plans. I'm doing shit. I'm not gonna be a stupid-ass stereotype like you.
DEVONTE	Don't call me that, Nicole.

He takes a deep breath.

               I'm trying.

NICOLE   Not hard enough. Make plans, set goals. Like, where do you see yourself in the next three years?

DEVONTE   Three years? I can't think that far ahead. Today was hectic enough.

NICOLE   Do you think you're gonna get old?

DEVONTE   What?

NICOLE   Do you see yourself getting old?

DEVONTE   What kind of a question is that?

NICOLE   It's a question. Can you see yourself with grey hair and a bald spot, playing dominoes in the park, telling stories about how you used to think you knew it all?

Silence.

               I want to see you get old.

DEVONTE   You do?

NICOLE   I do.

Silence.

               "When you want something, all the universe conspires in helping you to achieve it."

DEVONTE   That's pretty deep.

NICOLE   Paulo Coelho.

DEVONTE   How many of those quotes you got in that head of yours?

Pause.

Honestly, Nicole, it's kinda hard to make plans when you didn't even see yourself getting this far.

She holds his hand.

NICOLE*'s phone rings.*

NICOLE   Hello? What? You can't be serious.

Sighs.

Okay. Where? Okay.

She hangs up.

DEVONTE   What happened?
NICOLE   Shevon's been arrested.

SCENE 14

NICOLE *is waiting outside of a Toronto police station holding a shopping bag. Her exhaustion has reached new heights.* SHEVON *enters. They hug.*

NICOLE   Here.

> NICOLE *passes* SHEVON *a bag. She looks inside.*

SHEVON   Oh thank God.

> SHEVON *sits down and begins pulling out the items and putting them on or using them: extremely large hoop earrings; gel and a soft brush to pull her hair back in a slicked ponytail; a pocket mirror she uses to apply eyelash curler, eyeliner, mascara and lip gloss. They talk as she is doing these things.*

NICOLE	You okay?
SHEVON	Not really. But I'll figure it out. Thanks, boo.

NICOLE nods.

Where'd you get the money? You didn't ask my parents for it, did you?

NICOLE shakes her head.

NICOLE	Nah, I borrowed it from Devonte.
SHEVON	Good. Wait, since when does Devonte have money?
NICOLE	Shut up, Shevon.
SHEVON	I'm just saying—
NICOLE	They did call me though.
SHEVON	Who?
NICOLE	Your parents.
SHEVON	They did? What did they say?
NICOLE	They asked me if I'd heard from you.
SHEVON	What did you say?
NICOLE	I said no.
SHEVON	Good.
NICOLE	I think you should call them.
SHEVON	Nah man. I can't handle that right now.
NICOLE	It doesn't have to be a big thing, just let them know you're okay.
SHEVON	I don't want to talk to them.
NICOLE	Shevy—
SHEVON	Man, Nicole, leave it alone! What would I say to them? I wouldn't even know where to begin.

I can't handle . . . just . . . I'll pay Devonte
back. I promise.

Pause.

Did you call Winston?

NICOLE   I did.

SHEVON   And?

NICOLE   He didn't answer.

SHEVON   You left a message?

NICOLE   Yes.

SHEVON   And a text?

NICOLE   Yes.

SHEVON   Nothing? How did I end up here, Nicole?
I really thought he loved me. I've actually
become that girl. I'm so stupid.

NICOLE   You're not stupid.

SHEVON   Yes I am. I put everything on the line for him.
And now . . .

NICOLE   Iyanla Vanzant would say, "Forgive yourself
for believing that you're anything less than
beautiful."

SHEVON rolls her eyes and smiles.

SHEVON   That's actually a good one.

*NICOLE's phone rings. She looks at it and
then puts it back in her pocket.*

Was that him?

NICOLE	Nah, just some stupid private number that's been ringing down my phone all day. You already know I don't answer private.
SHEVON	It might be Winston though, calling from a different phone.
NICOLE	Shevon, he's the reason you're here.
SHEVON	Nah it's because I was slippin.
NICOLE	He's the reason you're slippin! He ain't calling.

Her phone rings again.

SHEVON	Please Nikki, just answer it!

NICOLE answers the phone.

NICOLE	Hello? . . . Yeah, who is this? . . . I told you before, don't call my number— What? . . . When? . . . I don't believe you. Where? . . . Yo, who the hell do you think you're— Yeah eh? You got talks? Watch when I see you. Come bring those talks to my face.

Hangs up.

SHEVON	Who was that?
NICOLE	That little trick Reneisha.
SHEVON	Reneisha from Rex?
NICOLE	Nah Reneisha from Jungs.
SHEVON	Oh that ho.
NICOLE	Yeah that ho.
SHEVON	What was she saying?

NICOLE   She said she was with Devonte last night.

Pause.

SHEVON   You think it's true?

Pause.

NICOLE   I don't know.

A beat.

SHEVON   So let's pull a mission.

SHEVON starts taking off her earrings.

NICOLE   Shevon. You just got out.
SHEVON   So? You're my girl. If you need me to ride,
         let's ride.

Pause.

NICOLE   Hold on.

NICOLE takes a few deep breaths.

         Nah . . . She's not the problem. Devonte is.
SHEVON   True. So let's go deal with his case.
NICOLE   Imma deal with him myself. Good looking out
         though.
SHEVON   Anytime.

Pause.

You okay?

NICOLE   I don't know. It's just a lot. It's like one thing after another. I'm drowning in this shit.

SHEVON   Nicole. It's gonna be okay.

NICOLE   Is it?

Pause.

Shit. I gotta go pick up Zakiya.

SHEVON   I can go get him. Where is he?

NICOLE   By Miss Irene's.

SHEVON   I thought you didn't want to leave him there.

NICOLE   Where the hell else was I supposed to leave him?

SHEVON   Okay, chill. I'll get him. I got you.

SCENE 15

It is the day of the march and people are gathering in front of the Movement offices. AKILAH is packing supplies for the protest. ELDER enters.

ELDER   Aki-wah!

AKILAH   My name is Akilah.

ELDER   Yes, yes. The police just came and told me that they have not been briefed on the route of the march.

AKILAH   And?

ELDER   And? Is this your first time organizing a rally? You have to brief the police on the route you are taking!

AKILAH   Why?

ELDER   What do you mean why? So they can block the roads!

AKILAH   We don't need them to block the roads. There are over seven hundred people here. We can block the roads on our own.

ELDER	But that's not how it's done—
AKILAH	It doesn't make any sense to brief the police on the route of a protest that is being organized against police brutality. What business is it of theirs what direction we take? If they weren't killing our people, we wouldn't need to be here.
ELDER	You are not being strategic about this!

BEVERLY enters.

BEVERLY	Sister Akilah!
AKILAH	If you'll please excuse me, Elder.

ELDER exits grumbling.

Hey! Ready for your speech?

BEVERLY	I suppose so. I'm so nervous my armpits are sweating.

AKILAH laughs.

AKILAH	You'll be fine.
BEVERLY	I wish my butterflies believed you.
AKILAH	How is the sign painting going?
BEVERLY	Great! Josiah's basically the next Jacob Lawrence.
AKILAH	He loves getting in on the action.
BEVERLY	He and Simba are just giving them the finishing touches by the bench.
AKILAH	Good.
BEVERLY	How are you?

AKILAH	Anxious. Excited. And good. Thank you for . . . always asking.
BEVERLY	Anytime. Do you by any chance know what time I go up?
AKILAH	I'm not sure. Check in with Khalil. He finalized the agenda last night.
BEVERLY	Do you know where he is?
AKILAH	Just follow the sound of the bullhorn. You know that man loves a microphone.

They laugh and then stop when KHALIL *enters with a clipboard and bullhorn under his arm.*

I'm gonna check on Josiah.

AKILAH *exits.*

BEVERLY	Brother Khalil!

BEVERLY *walks over to* KHALIL, *who is preoccupied with his clipboard.*

KHALIL	Ahh. Beverly, I was just looking for you.
BEVERLY	Great minds think alike.
KHALIL	Hm.
BEVERLY	I just wanted to check in and find out what time exactly I go up.
KHALIL	I need you to bring water for the speakers, and find the duct tape. We're also missing some placards—the red, black and green ones demanding justice—I think they may be in the

basement. Can you look for them? We'll be marching out soon.

BEVERLY   Oh, sure. But . . . when do I go up?

KHALIL   Go up where?

BEVERLY   To the podium.

KHALIL   The podium for what?

BEVERLY   To do my speech.

KHALIL   Your speech?

BEVERLY   Yes. The one you told me to write for today.

KHALIL   Oh. Beverly, we don't have time for that. We're already behind schedule.

AKILAH and ELDER re-enter looking at a clipboard.

BEVERLY   But . . . I've been preparing for weeks . . .

KHALIL   Beverly, are you seriously having a diva moment right now?

BEVERLY   Is this because of the other night?

KHALIL   What other night?

BEVERLY   I just thought—

KHALIL   You want me to delay the march so that you can satisfy your ego?

BEVERLY   You're talking to me about ego?

KHALIL   What?

BEVERLY   I'm sorry. I just can't—

KHALIL raises his voice so that everyone can here.

KHALIL   This is exactly the kind of self-centred individualistic mentality that destroys movements from

within. You need to check yourself and your
ego and remember why we are doing this work
and what the larger purpose is.

BEVERLY   I didn't join the movement to liberate Black
men only.

KHALIL   Who do you think you're—

AKILAH   What's going on?

KHALIL   Check yourself, Sister Beverly, and get it
together.

KHALIL and ELDER exit.

AKILAH   What just happened?

BEVERLY   Ummm . . . apparently we're running late
and . . . there isn't time for me to . . .

AKILAH sighs.

AKILAH   Are you okay?

BEVERLY   Yeah. I'm fine. I just have to . . . get the water
and the signs . . .

AKILAH   Don't worry about that.

BEVERLY   But Khalil said—

AKILAH   Forget what Khalil said. Let's march together.

*AKILAH hooks her arm through BEVERLY's
and they begin walking together. Suddenly
a crash is heard. People are yelling. There
is the sound of a police siren. KHALIL and
ELDER rush in.*

KHALIL	The police are starting to arrest people. You better get Josiah out of here.
AKILAH	Okay. You should go too.
ELDER	She's right. I'll stay here and try to calm things down.
BEVERLY	I'll call the legal team.

> *They all exchange looks and then exit in opposite directions.*

SCENE 16

DEVONTE enters. He is at the basketball court sitting on the bench, counting a wad of cash.

NICOLE *(from offstage)* Devonte! I need to talk to you!

DEVONTE Okay baby, give me a second.

NICOLE No, we need to talk right now!

NICOLE enters.

DEVONTE Nicole, I already told you, don't be bawlin' out my name on road like that.

NICOLE Where were you last night?

DEVONTE I told you. I was working.

NICOLE And I told you I'm not a dumb bitch. If you were working then why is Reneisha calling down my phone? Huh?

DEVONTE 'Cause's she's a dumb ho. She's just tryna get in your head.

NICOLE Don't try to play me Devonte.

DEVONTE	Yo, you need to calm down.
NICOLE	Don't tell me to calm down. I see these hos circling you now that you made a little change and I see you feeling too nice in yourself to tell them to slow their roll and step the fuck back.
DEVONTE	You're talking a lot of shit right now.
NICOLE	Mmmm-hmm. I'm talking shit. I'm just crazy right?
DEVONTE	Yo, why are you getting so dramatic? This ain't no R&B song.
NICOLE	How can I not be dramatic when you can't stop being a stupid-ass stereotype.
DEVONTE	I told you don't call me that.
NICOLE	Stereotype.
DEVONTE	Yo fam, I don't even know why I'm taking this right now when you're the one— Never mind.
NICOLE	When I what?
DEVONTE	Forget it.
NICOLE	You have something on your mind? Say it.
DEVONTE	All you do is nag me and tell me what I'm not doing, coming up with fictitious tales, spitting bare drama in my ear. You know what I'm doing? I'm helping you pay your bills. I'm helping your homegirls get out of jail. I'm putting up with your stupid quotes and vision posters—
NICOLE	Boards! It's a vision board! And it's not stupid!
DEVONTE	Board, poster, whatever! I'm taking care of the kid you decided to have while I was putting in work for us—
NICOLE	What? I didn't hear from you for two years! What "us" is there when you don't call, write, text, email, anything—

DEVONTE	Well differently, I'm here now.
NICOLE	Yeah. You're here now. Fucking around.
DEVONTE	You know what? You're the one who's not putting weight in.
NICOLE	Excuse me?
DEVONTE	You heard me. You're the one who's not down.
NICOLE	I'm not down? You're telling me that I'm not down? Tell me how I, the woman who bailed you out of jail—
DEVONTE	Please—
NICOLE	—is not down.
DEVONTE	First of all, you bailed me out with my own money 'cause I paid you back, so don't even come with that.
NICOLE	Wow, so that's how you're moving now?
DEVONTE	And second of all . . . I wasn't even tryin to bring none of this up but now that you acting all wild I'll just say it.
NICOLE	Say what?
DEVONTE	The last time I came out, you should have had my money ready for me and my clothes all sorted out and shit.
NICOLE	Are you serious right now?
DEVONTE	Yeah yo. That's just basic shit.
NICOLE	Basic for who? I'm sorry, I must have skipped the class on what to do when dating jailbirds.
DEVONTE	And on top of that, the whole time I was inside you were mad inconsistent with the canteen.
NICOLE	Wow. Mans want to talk about the canteen eh?
DEVONTE	Yeah I'm talking about the canteen.
NICOLE	Okay let's talk about it then. I'm not gonna go all out for you with my hard-earned legit

money because I'm not dumb. I know you have next girls that were stocking your canteen.

DEVONTE   Psshh.

NICOLE   You have two visits every week . . .

DEVONTE   Here we go . . .

NICOLE   . . . and I'm the one who brings your mom there, so who's the other visit? Huh? Three weeks in a row. Who's the other girl?

DEVONTE   We already discussed this. I'm not going over old shit. All you really need to know . . .

NICOLE   Tell me what I need to know.

DEVONTE   . . . is "the other girl" had shit ready for me and she ain't even my girl. I'm calling you, you're my girl, but it's the next chick that has the Jordans and the telly ready for me when I get out.

NICOLE   That's what you're concerned about? Jordans? That's how you define who's down for you? Yo fuck your Jordans and fuck you.

DEVONTE   Yo, relax on my Jordans.

NICOLE   Why are you even locked up in the first place?

DEVONTE   Nicole, I'm not in the mood for no life lecture.

NICOLE   Well I'm not in the mood for some ho to be calling down my phone!

DEVONTE   So then change your number!

NICOLE   Okaaay. I see you. Mans feeling too nice right now. Cyatties calling my phone like I'm some side chick. Tryna humiliate me. But karma is a bitch and this shit don't ever last.

NICOLE pulls out tattered rags from her bag and throws them at DEVONTE.

DEVONTE	What the—yo . . . is that my Avirex jacket? Nicole. Is that my leather Avirex jacket?
NICOLE	I think the more accurate statement is that it *was* your leather Avirex jacket. I told you not to fuck with me.

Silence.

DEVONTE	Get out of my face.
NICOLE	Or what?
DEVONTE	I'm not gonna tell you again, Nicole!
NICOLE	I'm so tired of this shit.

She begins walking away.

DEVONTE	So what now, you're leaving me? Again?
NICOLE	You're the one that left!
DEVONTE	You're the one who went and had a kid with someone else!

Pause.

	I thought you were my ride-or-die.
NICOLE	You gotta take in the other side of the game Devonte. Don't I deserve loyalty? Don't I deserve more than this?

SHEVON enters running.

SHEVON	Nicole!
NICOLE	Where's Zakiya?
SHEVON	I'm so sorry.

NICOLE	Where is Zakiya, Shevon?
SHEVON	Someone called the cops on Miss Irene. Told them she was running an unlicensed nursery.
NICOLE	Oh my God.
SHEVON	CAS came. They took all the kids . . .
NICOLE	Oh my God.
DEVONTE	Nicole—

The police are heard. NICOLE *and* DEVONTE *look at each other.*

Nicole—

NICOLE	Go!

DEVONTE *runs off and* NICOLE *and* SHEVON *exit in the opposite direction.*

SCENE 17

AKILAH and BEVERLY *are back at the office for the Movement.*

BEVERLY   I started drafting the statement for the press. Khalil just wanted to look it over. I'm not sure if you do too . . .

AKILAH   No, that's fine. This afternoon I'll call members on the secure line to coordinate the debrief. We'll need to have a strong presence at the hearings.

Pause.

Beverly, I'm sorry you didn't get to do your speech.

BEVERLY   It's fine.

AKILAH   It's not fine.

BEVERLY   I just don't get why he . . . I don't know. Maybe it's my fault.

AKILAH	It's not.
BEVERLY	I guess I was naive after all.
AKILAH	No. It's my fault. I didn't prepare you for the other side of all this. It won't always be like this.
BEVERLY	Are you sure about that?

Pause.

AKILAH	You wrote a speech. You were denied your right to have your speech heard. That's not okay. Maybe . . . maybe you could do it now.
BEVERLY	Now?
AKILAH	Yeah. Why not? Do it now. For me. I want to hear it.
BEVERLY	Really?
AKILAH	Really.

They smile at each other. BEVERLY stands up and takes a piece of paper from a file folder.

| BEVERLY | Good afternoon, comrades. Today we mark— |

ELDER rushes in.

ELDER	Akilah! Khalil's been arrested.
AKILAH	What?
ELDER	The police attacked him a couple of hours ago when he left Third World Books. Kwame has disappeared. They picked up Simba at her house this morning. Brother Jamal told me to tell you that they're looking for you next.

BEVERLY	Shit.
ELDER	We have to get you out of here. Now. They'll be here any minute.
AKILAH	But Josiah. I have to get him first.
BEVERLY	Where is he?
AKILAH	At home. My aunt's watching him.
ELDER	There is no time.
AKILAH	What are you talking about? I'm not leaving without my son.
ELDER	We can't get you to the other side of the city to a location where the police will inevitably be waiting. You have to go underground now.

Silence. AKILAH *is in shock.*

BEVERLY	She's coming. She'll meet you outside.
ELDER	We don't have time!
BEVERLY	Two minutes!

ELDER *exits.*

	Akilah? Akilah. Say something.
AKILAH	Josiah . . .
BEVERLY	It will only be temporary. You just have to go underground for a bit.
AKILAH	My son . . .
BEVERLY	He'll be fine. I'll take care of him. Akilah.
AKILAH	But he's my son.
BEVERLY	I know, but you have to go. How can you help him if you're behind bars? Akilah. Akilah, look at me.

AKILAH	They'll try to get Children's Aid . . . Oh my God . . . I can't do this . . .
BEVERLY	Yes you can. I won't let them take him.
AKILAH	You have to tell him I'll be back to get him.
BEVERLY	I will.
AKILAH	You promise?
BEVERLY	I promise. I've got it all under control. I'll hide all of the files. I'll call the lawyers and the other chapters, I'll—
AKILAH	Yes, but my son! Josiah . . .
BEVERLY	I'll tell him that you love him and that you will be coming to get him soon. Because you will.
AKILAH	He won't understand.

They embrace. AKILAH begins to walk out and then stops.

Thank you.

AKILAH exits and BEVERLY sits down, lost in her thoughts.

SCENE 18

BEVERLY and NICOLE are sitting in the visitors' waiting room of the Don Jail. Both are pissed off and impatient.

GUARD   Numbers forty-four, sixty-three, fifty-seven, forty-eight and seventy.

BEVERLY and NICOLE rise to face the guard.

Ma'am?

NICOLE   I've been waiting for three hours. Why is it taking you so long to find him?

GUARD   What's your number?

NICOLE &
BEVERLY   Number thirty-nine.

GUARD   That number has not been called yet.

BEVERLY   I know that. I'm asking you why.

GUARD   There are a number of reasons why this may be the case. Take a seat. We will call your number when the inmate is brought in.

BEVERLY	I've been sitting. I've been waiting. It's been three hours. Is there something wrong?
GUARD	Nothing is wrong. This is simply standard procedure. Your number will be called.
NICOLE	This is crazy! How is it taking this long? Did you lose him? Do you not know where he his? Did you forget?
GUARD	Ma'am, please don't raise your voice.
BEVERLY	I just don't understand why I am sitting here watching lawyers and guards and counsellors walking through the door so easily while I just have to wait?
NICOLE	Are we not important?
BEVERLY	Do we not matter?
GUARD	Ma'am . . .
NICOLE	I made sure to come early, I came early because I recognize that my time here is limited. It has a start time and an end time.
BEVERLY	So now this is my time: Why aren't you guys hurrying up?
NICOLE	You work here. You get paid to be here. What is the problem?
GUARD	Numbers eighty-one, seventy-nine, eighty-seven, ninety-four and thirty-nine.

Both women smile triumphantly at the guard.
KHALIL *enters and sits in a chair.* BEVERLY *sits across from him.*

BEVERLY	Hello.
KHALIL	Hello. Thank you for coming, Beverly. How are you?

BEVERLY	I'm . . . here. How are you?
KHALIL	I'm alive. Where is she?
BEVERLY	I can't say.
KHALIL	I guess that's for the best. Her son?
BEVERLY	Josiah's okay.
KHALIL	Good. Good. The Movement office?
BEVERLY	They raided it. I got all the crucial items out beforehand, but they stole or destroyed everything else.

KHALIL sighs.

KHALIL	I figured they would. Do you have any updates on my case?
BEVERLY	The lawyers are working on it but . . . it doesn't look good.

KHALIL nods. Silence.

KHALIL	They put me in solitary confinement.
BEVERLY	What? Why?
KHALIL	No special reason other than fearing I'll revolutionize the gen pop.
BEVERLY	I suppose that's a legitimate fear.

KHALIL chuckles grimly.

KHALIL	I'm okay now, I just . . . it's just . . . it's hard to get my thoughts together. It's good to see you. I know that—
BEVERLY	I've been able to keep weekend classes going. There aren't that many of us left but Elder

connected us with the Black Education Project. He wants to begin rebuilding the library next month.

KHALIL   Good. Good. Beverly, I wanted to say—

BEVERLY   We were able to disseminate a one-page news-letter updating the community on everything, but we don't have the resources to restart the newspaper. At least not yet.

KHALIL   Yes of course.

Pause.

I'm just having some trouble organizing . . . my thoughts . . . the smell, the rotten food . . . it's all just—

BEVERLY   I'll talk to the lawyers. Maybe we can issue a formal complaint.

KHALIL   Thank you. Beverly . . . I . . . I'm sorry for . . .

He does not finish his sentence and BEVERLY *does not help him to finish it.*

BEVERLY   I will help to arrange all the necessary docu-mentation for your trial.

KHALIL   Thank you—

BEVERLY   But I won't be coming back here for a while.

KHALIL   What? No. Beverly. You can't leave me here.

BEVERLY   I can't be everywhere. I promised Akilah I would take care of her son and he is my priority now.

KHALIL   No, Beverly, please.

BEVERLY   I'm going back to Halifax with him. It's what she wants. Toronto's not safe.

KHALIL	I can't do this alone.
BEVERLY	You're not alone. You have lawyers and activists working round the clock building a campaign. Elder has already said—
KHALIL	They'll forget about me. Everyone will forget . . .
BEVERLY	Khalil. No one will forget if you don't forget. Remember why you are here: you are here for defending your people. You are here because you are a revolutionary. You are here because you will not hesitate to die for our freedom. That's what you told me. It's time for me to define my own resistance. But know that they can never truly lock you up. Nothing and no one can stop this movement.
KHALIL	Beverly, I need you.
BEVERLY	No you don't. Akilah needs me. I need me. You have everything you need.
GUARD	Time's up.

BEVERLY leaves. DEVONTE sits in the chair across from NICOLE.

NICOLE	Hey.
DEVONTE	Hey. Damn. You look beautiful.
NICOLE	How are you doing?
DEVONTE	I'm alive.
NICOLE	Is . . . everything okay?
DEVONTE	It's fine. Don't worry about me. How's Zakiya?
NICOLE	He's okay. He's back home.
DEVONTE	Good, good. What's going on wit you?
NICOLE	Listen, Devonte, I just came 'cause you called and . . .

DEVONTE	I know . . .
NICOLE	You didn't sound so good on the phone and . . .
DEVONTE	I'm sorry. I shouldn't have . . . I didn't mean to worry you.
NICOLE	What happened?
DEVONTE	Nothin. You know how they are. They were just waiting to pick me up for some dumb shit.

Silence.

Say something.

| NICOLE | What is there to say? |

They sit in silence.

DEVONTE	I just needed to see you 'cause . . . this shit's gonna sound crazy but . . . yo, the devil's always talking to me. The devil's always talking to me in here.
NICOLE	What do you mean?
DEVONTE	It's just . . . all these voices like . . . they're from another time . . . a memory but . . . I dunno, shit's hectic, man . . .
NICOLE	Did you talk to someone about it? A doctor or something? . . .
DEVONTE	They just moved me to this special unit.
NICOLE	What special unit?
DEVONTE	I dunno . . . a special unit . . . for people who hear voices or something . . .
NICOLE	What?
DEVONTE	It makes me feel like I'm f'real crazy.
NICOLE	You should see a shrink, not be put in some . . .

DEVONTE   It's cool . . . I'll be fine . . . Nicole . . . I'll be fine . . . I just . . . I just needed to see you. I'm sorry for . . .

He doesn't finish and NICOLE *doesn't help him.*

Can you come back?

Silence.

Please. Nicole. I need you.
NICOLE   You don't need me.
DEVONTE   I do. I can't do this without you. Please?

DEVONTE *puts his hand up to the glass. After a pause* NICOLE *does the same.*

I'm sorry.
NICOLE   No one can save you when you don't love yourself enough to be your own saviour.
DEVONTE   Damn. Who was that? Paulo or Iyanla?
NICOLE   That was me.
GUARD   Time's up.

All exit. The waiting room is empty.

Numbers forty-two, twenty-three, eight, and three.

Lights out.

ACKNOWLEDGEMENTS

Kevin, Mum, Keisha-Monique, Tsegai, Cahoots Theatre
Company, Obsidian Theatre Company, Marjorie, the Hot
House participants, the Piece of Mine Festival, the rock.
paper.sistahz Festival, all the actors of every workshop,
reading and staging, all the interviewees, all the contrib-
utors to The Ride or Die Project blog, the Toronto Arts
Council, the Ontario Arts Council, the Canada Council
for the Arts, the Michaëlle Jean Foundation, Quentin,
Muginga, Odeen, Roots Redemption, the Parris family, the
Hood family and the chosen family.

By day, Amanda Parris is a television and radio host and writes a weekly column. By night, she writes stories for the stage and screen. *Other Side of the Game* is her first published play. In Amanda's past lives she was an educator who wrote arts-based curricula, attended numerous acting auditions and dreamed of opening a school that Blue Ivy Carter would attend. Over the course of her career, Amanda has worn a variety of hats, working as an educator, a researcher, an actor and a community organizer. She is the co-founder of the award-winning alternative education organization Lost Lyrics and worked with the Remix Project and the Manifesto Festival. She has spoken about her work at United Nations conferences around the world. Parris completed her Honours B.A. degree in Political Science and Women's Studies at York University and her M.A. degree in Sociology of Education at the University of Toronto. She was a playwright-in-residence at Cahoots Theatre Company and Alameda Theatre Company and studied writing and acting at b current performing arts, anitafrika dub theatre and the Lee Strasberg Theatre & Film Institute.

First edition: May 2019. Second printing: March 2020.
Printed and bound in Canada by Rapido Books, Montreal

Author photo © CJ Cromwell
Jacket art by Alexis Eke
Jacket design by Joseph Stephen Gatto

**PLAYWRIGHTS
CANADA PRESS**

202-269 Richmond St. W.
Toronto, ON
M5V 1X1

416.703.0013
info@playwrightscanada.com
www.playwrightscanada.com
@playcanpress